The Financial Data Playbook

Chris Conlan

Contents

The Financial Data Playbook
Chris Conlan
Charlotte, North Carolina
USA

ISBN-13: 9798534050783

About the Author

Chris Conlan is the founder and CEO of Conlan Scientific, a financial data science consultancy based out of Charlotte, North Carolina. He works with his team of data scientists to build machine learning solutions for banks, lenders, investors, traders, and fintech companies. Chris holds a Bachelor's in Statistics from the University of Virginia, where he later co-taught a data science capstone course.

About the Technical Contributors

Cullen Baker is a financial data scientist at Conlan Scientific. He has experience working as both a proprietary trader and a machine learning engineer. He holds a Bachelor's in Mathematics from Clemson as well as a Masters in Financial Engineering from NYU and a Masters in Data Science from UVA.

Alex Bartlett is the director of strategic advisory at Conlan Scientific. Prior to joining Conlan, she spent four years in Barclays' investment banking division. She graduated with honors and distinction from the University of Iowa, where she received a B.B.A. in Finance and a B.S.E. in Chemical Engineering.

Katherine Sylvester is a financial data scientist at Conlan Scientific. She leverages her extensive statistics and computer science education to implement modern data analysis techniques. She is currently pursuing a B.S. in Statistics and Data Science at Yale.

Preface

Six years ago, I founded Conlan Scientific. Since then, I have worked with many different businesses to solve many different financial data challenges.

Our clients span the financial services industry, but they are primarily investors and lenders. They are all putting investment capital to work in an effort to make a superior risk-adjusted return.

At Conlan Scientific, we write a lot of computer code. In this book, I will not focus on code. Instead, I will focus on business lessons I have learned over the years, and I will express them as mathematical arguments. These business lessons form the basis of many real-life discussions I have with our clients. I hope that readers will find them helpful, enjoyable, and thought-provoking.

Chris Conlan

Chapter 1

Investing in Accuracy

Data scientists want to build prediction models with a high level of accuracy. Executives want to invest in projects with a high return on investment. This chapter will attempt to establish a relationship between the accuracy of machine learning models and the rate of return on investing operations. Ultimately, it will help you understand when and how it can make sense to invest in financial data projects.

The following discussion is mathematically general and applies to any financial services company that invests or loans money, including, for example, mutual funds, banks, and real estate developers.

1.1 Definitions

The following section sets up a mathematical model for discussing the circumstances under which it is appropriate to invest in financial data projects based on their ability to improve investment performance.

1.1.1   Equity Curve and Internal Rate of Return

Suppose that a financial services business holds both investments and cash. The investments are in a portfolio with a total value represented by P_t. The amount of the business's cash is represented by C_t. We will measure the performance of the business's investments in financial data projects by measuring the change in the equity curve E_t at $t \in 1, ..., T$.

$$E_t = C_t + P_t$$

We treat $E_0 = C_0$ as the starting capital, and we define ΔE_t as follows, and similarly for C_t and P_t.

$$\Delta E_t = E_t - E_{t-1}$$

Our primary measure of performance will be the Internal Rate of Return (IRR), represented by r_I, which is calculated by numerically solving the following equation.

$$\sum_{t=1}^{T} \frac{\Delta E_t}{(1 + r_I)^{t-1}} = 0$$

In practice, one unit of t can represent any amount of time based on the investment scenario being studied.

We assume that all transacting and rebalancing happens instantaneously at time t, and all changes in equity and portfolio value due to changes in market prices of assets occur from t to $t + 1$.

t	C_t	P_t	E_t	ΔE_t	r_t
0	1000	0	1000		
1	200	820	1020	20	0.02
2	200	880	1080	60	0.059
3	200	850	1050	-30	-0.028
4	200	900	1100	50	0.048

Table 1.1: Example equity curve behavior for investing in assets

For analytic simplicity, we will frequently consider the following scenario.

- T goes to ∞.
- ΔE_t is a constant positive number, ΔE_c, for $t > 1$
- ΔE_1 is a negative number representing the amount of a single upfront expense.

In this scenario, r_I has a closed-form solution provided by the known properties of infinite geometric series.

$$r_I = -\frac{\Delta E_c}{\Delta E_1} = \frac{\Delta E_c}{\Delta E_1{}'}$$

If we define $\Delta E_1{}' = -\Delta E_1$ in order to treat the upfront cost as a positive number, the IRR formula reduces to something resembling the vanilla return on investment (ROI) formula, where $\Delta E_1{}'$ represents the invested capital and ΔE_c represents the profit on the investment.

t	C_t	P_t	E_t	ΔE_t	r_t
0	1000	0	1000		
1	800	0	800	-200	-0.2
2	0	880	880	80	0.1
3	0	960	960	80	0.091
4	0	1040	1040	80	0.083
∞	0	∞	∞	80	≈ 0

Table 1.2: Example equity curve behavior for R&D investment with constant payout

See Table 1.2 for an example equity curve for research and development costs where the upfront investment is $E_1 = -200$ and constant return is $E_c = 80$. In this example, the r_I is 40%. From $t = 0$ to $t = 1$ the change reflects investing \$200 of the available capital in R&D. Then, from $t = 1$ to $t = 2$, the remaining \$800 is invested in a portfolio that begins making the return of E_c. Note how the IRR depends solely on the payback from R&D, not the capital investment required to run the portfolio.

We will also consider the following trivial scenario.

- $t \in 0, 1, 2.$ $T = 2$.
- ΔE_1 is a negative number representing the amount of a single upfront investment.
- ΔE_2 is a positive number representing the one-time return from the investment.

In this scenario, r_I reduces to the formula for return on investment (ROI).

$$r_I = \frac{\Delta E_2}{\Delta E_1{}'} - 1$$

See Table 1.3 for an example equity curve for a single payout investment involving research and development costs of $E_1 = -500$ and a one-time return of $E_2 = 250$. In this example, the r_I is 50%. Note how from $t = 0$ to $t = 1$ the change reflects investing \$500 of the available capital in R&D. Then, from $t = 1$ to $t = 2$, the remaining $500 is invested in a portfolio that makes a one-time return of $250. Note how the IRR depends solely on the expenses and the payback, not the capital investment required to generate the payback.

t	C_t	P_t	E_t	ΔE_t	r_t
0	1000	0	1000		
1	500	0	500	-500	-0.5
2	0	750	750	250	0.5

Table 1.3: Example equity curve behavior of single payout

With these definitions settled, we will proceed to integrate the notion of predictive accuracy into our mathematical model.

1.1.2 Financial Agents, Prediction Models, and Accuracy

Assume that the business employs some number of financial agents that are responsible for making and managing investments on behalf of the business. The business incurs a cost for employing these agents, in the form of salaries, with the aim of profiting from their investment expertise. They predict the outcomes of potential investment opportunities with a certain accuracy, R_A^2, which represents the standardized mean squared error, or *R-squared*, of the agents' predictions. The R-squared accuracy, or just the *accuracy*, for the purposes of our discussion, is a number typically bounded from below at 0 and always bounded from above at 1, where 0 represents a set of uninformed predictions, and 1 represents a set of flawless predictions.

The R-squared accuracy is not typically used to evaluate investment management performance, because that would require that we evaluate the accuracy of predictions on investments that were not made. In certain industries, and for a number of asset types, this is an impossible task. Nonetheless, for our discussion, we will model the accuracy of predictions made by financial agents, for investments they both made and did not make, for the purpose of comparing them to the predictions made by machine learning models. Machine learning models typically use R-squared as a measure of accuracy, so it is necessary to measure the agents' accuracy in these terms to establish a common performance metric. We will proceed with a definition of R-squared.

Given a set of n investment opportunities, $i \in 1, ..., n$, each has an outcome y_i and a predicted outcome of $\hat{y}_i$. The *error* of the outcome is represented as $y_i - \hat{y}_i$ and the squared error is its square. The R-squared is the proportion of the variance of the random variable Y accounted for by the predictions. Given the sample mean, $\bar{y}$, of the random variable Y, the following is the most expository way of calculating R-squared.

$$R^2 = 1 - \frac{\sum_{i=1}^{n}(y_i - \hat{y}_i)^2}{\sum_{i=1}^{n}(y_i - \bar{y})^2}$$

In other words, the R-squared represents, typically on a scale of 0 to 1, how much better the model's predictions are than a naive prediction using the sample mean. In practice, there is nothing preventing the R-squared from being negative. If the predictions are on average worse than a naive prediction using the sample mean, then the R-squared will be negative.

The above R-squared formula applies to what are called *regression* problems in machine learning. Regression problems involve predicting the exact value of a random variable, like the price of a stock tomorrow. We will still use the term R-squared and the variable R^2 to refer to the prediction accuracy in classification problems, but the formula is different. It is as follows, where $\mathbb{1}[f(\cdot)]$ represents the indicator function, which returns the value 1 if the condition $f(\cdot)$ is true and 0 if it is false. This formulation is also referred to as the classification accuracy.

$$R^2 = \frac{1}{n} \sum_{i=1}^{n} \mathbb{1}[y_i \equiv \hat{y}_i]$$

We will move on to bridge these concepts in the context of financial machine learning projects within different types of organizations.

1.2 Market Makers

We will use a simple model of the business of a market maker for our first example. Market makers make frequent short-term trades. If an asset has a bid and an ask price, the market maker typically endeavors to buy at the bid and sell at the ask, potentially with a brief holding period, to make a small profit. They aim to do this many times per day over many assets to produce a consistent stream of mostly profitable trades.

Readers may notice that the market maker's trading activities in our example sound very similar to those of a high-frequency trading shop. This is intentional, and the discussion that follows can also apply to high-frequency traders.

For simplicity, we will assume that all the trades made by the market maker are of equal initial dollar value. We will model the returns on these trades as a random normal variable $X \sim \mathcal{N}(\mu, \sigma^2)$ with $\mu = 0$. The market makers, acting as financial agents of the business, will be responsible for predicting whether or not X is positive or negative, and they will take the appropriate position (long or short) based on this prediction. In other words, the market makers will predict Y, which is the sign of X, with accuracy R_A^2, and trade the assets accordingly. The percentage return on trade i can be represented as $x_i * \hat{y}_i$.

To calculate how this trading behavior affects the equity of the business, E_t, we need to make some assumptions about how money is managed within the market making business. We will assume that the firm makes m investments per period t each with $C_m = C_0/m$ dollars. We assume this is the invested amount per trade regardless of the prior day's performance or cash balance, C_t. All gains or losses from trading will be represented as changes to the cash balance ΔC_t. The portfolio will be liquidated before the end of each period, meaning that $P_t = 0$ and $E_t = C_t$ throughout.

Given that m_t is the set of all trades made between $t - 1$ and t, the component of ΔE_t attributable to trading activities is as follows.

$$C_m \sum_{i \in m_t} x_i * \hat{y}_i$$

By separating the winning trades from the losing trades, we can start to see how predictive accuracy affects performance of the business and the IRR.

Since X is normally distributed with $\mu = 0$, the mean of $|X|$ is $\sqrt{\frac{2}{\pi}}\sigma = \gamma\sigma \approx 0.798 * \sigma$. We can use this fact to start to separate out the effects of correct and incorrect predictions. Given the set of m_t^+ correct predictions and m_t^- incorrect predictions, the above equation can be expressed as follows.

$$C_m \left(\sum_{i \in m_t^+} |x_i| - \sum_{i \in m_t^-} |x_i| \right)$$

Given that m_t^+ has $R_A^2 m$ elements, m_t^- has $1 - R_A^2 m$ elements, and the mean of $|X|$ is $\gamma\sigma$, the expected impact on ΔE_t from trading activities can be expressed as such.

$$C_m \left(R_A^2 m \gamma \sigma - (1 - R_A^2) m \gamma \sigma \right)$$

Reducing the expression further, we get this very brief expression for the expected gains or losses from trading activities.

$$\mathbb{E}[\Delta E_t] = C_0 \gamma \sigma \left(2 R_A^2 - 1 \right)$$

The above expression tells us that the profit or loss of the market making business is a function of the invested cash, the volatility of the traded assets, and the prediction accuracy. The maximum expected profit or loss is $C_0 \gamma \sigma$ with perfectly accurate or perfectly inaccurate predictions, respectively.

If we treat $\Delta E_t / C_0$ as the return on invested capital and σ as proportional to the volatility of the overall portfolio, then we can assert that the Sharpe Ratio, ϕ, is proportional to $2 R_A^2 - 1$, the zero-centered accuracy of predictions. To arrive at this result, we define the Sharpe Ratio as follows,

$$r_t = \frac{\Delta E_t}{C_0} \qquad r_a = \frac{E_T - C_0}{C_0} * \frac{1}{T} \qquad r_b = 0$$

where r_a is the annualized return, r_b is the benchmark return, and σ_{r_t} is the volatility of returns r_t. We set the benchmark return r_b to zero because the trading activity is necessarily high-frequency, meaning there is no reasonable risk-free or passive return to which we can associate the strategy. Given that the invested amount is constant at C_0, we use the arithmetic mean of returns for r_a in order to simplify the math.

$$\phi = \frac{r_a - r_b}{\sigma_{r_t}}$$

To further our argument, we will derive an expression for $\mathbb{E}[E_T]$ in terms of the above.

$$E_T = C_0 + \sum_{t=1}^{T} \Delta E_t$$

$$\mathbb{E}[E_T] = C_0 + T\mathbb{E}[\Delta E_t]$$

If we assume that σ is proportional to the volatility of the overall portfolio, we can substitute σ for σ_{r_t}. By replacing E_T with $\mathbb{E}[E_T]$ in the Sharpe Ratio equation, we get the following.

$$\phi = \gamma(2R_A^2 - 1)$$

This is a powerful assertion. The Sharpe Ratio is directly proportional to the zero-centered accuracy of predictions.

Readers will note that the maximum attainable Sharpe Ratio in this model is $\phi = \gamma$ for $R_A^2 = 1$. This is a consequence of our assumption of equal volatility in the market and in portfolio. To get the Sharpe Ratio above 0.8 in this trading model, the trader must reduce the portfolio risk relative to the market.

1.2.1 Interpretation and Discussion

Financial services professionals often discuss the meaning of *51% accuracy* as a way of expressing the simple fact that making a profit involves placing more winning bets than losing bets. As such, they may be unexcited to invest in projects that only marginally improve the accuracy of their predictions. Say, for example, that a market making firm employs a cabal of discretionary traders that place 52% winning bets. The firm makes money year after year and is comfortable with its operating procedures. Then, a hot shot analyst comes along and claims he can make a predictive model that has 53% accuracy. Should the firm invest time and money into the analyst's idea? This mathematical model provides a method for answering that question.

Consider that the firm in this example has \$1 billion in capital. Further, a unit increment in t represents the time it takes the firm to turn over \$1 billion in trading volume, which is once per hour during the NYSE trading day. The volatility of returns on these trades is 0.2% on average, and there are approximately 1,620 trading hours in a year. The firm makes a healthy \$104 million in trading gains each year with this business model and financial agents operating at $R_A^2 = 0.52$. If a new model delivers $R_B^2 = 0.53$, the firm's yearly trading gains would be \$156 million. For this firm, each percentage point gained in overall accuracy yields an additional \$52 million in trading gains and an additional 5.2% return on assets. Successful market making firms understand this, so they are in constant competition with each other to build the most accurate models and the most efficient execution pipelines.

Because there is such intense competition in the market making industry, models are rarely useful for more than 18 months. Assuming a typical model has a useful lifespan of 12 months, we should model a single upfront investment and a single payout when computing the IRR for R&D investments at high-frequency market making firms. The investment represents the year's R&D expenses for model development, and the payout represents the gains in accuracy accrued from the model developed in the previous year. Mathematically, this calculation is equivalent to a simple return on invested capital (ROIC) analysis.

The mathematical model we proposed here can be extended to any business allocating capital across a variety of equity assets. The only necessary adjustments would be to unit of t and the value of σ. We will extend this model further to different types of assets and different styles of investing.

1.3 Stock Pickers

In comparison to market makers, stock pickers have a fundamentally different problem to solve. Stock pickers are interested in only allocating money to a select few highly profitable opportunities. In other words, a stock picker's job is to make sure that, at each period in time t, out of all M possible investment opportunities, he has allocated capital to the m opportunities that he projects will make the most money.

Mathematically, this is an interesting proposition. For example, in a universe of 3,000 actively traded U.S. stocks, an investment manager that identifies the ten best performers each quarter will be very successful. He does not need to predict the performance of these stocks, nor does he need to rank these stocks. He just needs to identify them.

In this section, we will define the *mean average precision* in the context of stock picking. We will then express the Sharpe Ratio in terms of it. First, we will consider that the stock picker has the job of selecting m investments at time t, from a universe of M possible investments, that beat the benchmark return of r_b from t to $t+1$. The return on investment j from t to $t+1$ is defined as $r_{t,j}$. We also define $j \in M$ and $j \in J_t$, where J_t is the set of size m of the chosen investments at time t.

In machine learning terms, we are arguing that the stock picker only cares about precision, not recall. In other words, he is concerned with whether or not his stock picks outperform the market, rather than if he can pick all outperforming stocks. Precision is broadly defined as the number of true positive estimates divided by the number of all positive estimates. We will narrow this definition in the context of stock-picking ahead.

We will also argue that the stock picker only cares about precision for his top m stock picks. He does not care whether or not his least favored stock picks perform, because he will not be investing in them. Therefore, to measure the accuracy of his investment selections, we will use the *mean average precision* measured only on the top m stock picks. In other disciplines, this metric is typically referred to as the *mean average precision at k* and is often unattractively notated as $MAP@k$. We will denote this metric as μ_p.

Given the above definitions, we can write the precision of a single estimate as the following.

$$\mathbb{1}[r_{t,j} > r_b]$$

Given a set of m stock picks J_t, we can write the average precision as the following.

$$\frac{1}{m} \sum_{j \in J_t} \mathbb{1}[r_{t,j} > r_b]$$

For the purposes of calculating precision, m is considered to be the count of all true positives and all false positives. From here, we can define the mean average precision as the mean of the above expression over all $t \in 1, ..., T$.

$$\mu_p = \frac{1}{T * m} \sum_{t=1}^{T} \sum_{j \in J_t} \mathbb{1}[r_{t,j} > r_b]$$

The range of μ_p is 0 to 1, inclusive, and expresses the average proportion of good stock picks made by the investor. This formula allows us to compare the performance of many different stock-picking methodologies, including regression models, ad-hoc scoring systems, and traditional company screeners. In other words, as long a stock-picking methodology provides a means of calculating J_t, then this formula can evaluate its accuracy. From here, we will establish a relationship between μ_p and the Sharpe Ratio, ϕ.

We will model the returns on trades made by the stock picker as a random normal variable $X \sim \mathcal{N}(r_b, \sigma^2)$. Following a similar argument to the one we made about returns from market making activities, we can arrive at the expected change in the equity curve from investing activities at time t.

$$\mathbb{E}[\Delta E_t] = C_0(r_b + \gamma\sigma\left(2\mu_p - 1\right))$$

While the result is similar, the argument about stock pickers is fundamentally different, because it shows that precision μ_p within a ranking context is a meaningful substitute for model accuracy R_A^2. This is especially relevant in evaluating the efficacy of legacy scoring and ranking algorithms against potentially new machine learning solutions. In other words, if a budding analyst is proposing a new machine learning approach to supplant a legacy approach, he will have to beat the legacy method on the basis of μ_p if his solution is to be deemed valuable.

Following a similar argument to before, we can arrive at the following formula for the Sharpe Ratio, ϕ.

$$\phi = \gamma(2\mu_p - 1)$$

Even in the presence of a non-zero benchmark return r_b, the Sharpe Ratio equation simplifies to the exact same expression as with market makers.

In both of the previous examples, we placed a strict upper and lower bound on the Sharpe Ratio by forcing the portfolio volatility to be equal to the market volatility. There is additional opportunity to increase the Sharpe Ratio above $\gamma \approx 0.8$ by reducing the volatility of the portfolio relative to the market.

Chapter 2

Square Root Rule of Uncertainty

One of the most important underlying principles of applied statistics is what I call the *square root rule of uncertainty*. This rule applies to almost anything that utilizes standard deviations in its measurement, including confidence intervals, statistical power, translation of volatility, and composite random variables. This chapter will discuss some prime examples and attempt to imbue the user with some intuition about uncertainty. We will assume the reader has a basic understanding of the measurement of standard deviations.

2.1 Motivation

Given the frequency that the square root of the sample size, $\sqrt{n}$, appears in applied statistics, you might believe that there is nothing particularly special about it. However, the square root of the sample size is the key to answering one the most common business questions asked in the data science world: *How much data do I need?* Once you have acquired a data set and created a model, you will ask the question: *How much more data do I need?* The square root rule will help you answer these questions.

2.2   The Law of Large Numbers

The law of large numbers is as follows. Given a series of independent and identically distributed (i.i.d.) random variables x_i for $i \in 1, ..., n$, with a constant mean $\mu_{x_i} = \mu$, define the sample average $\bar{x}$ as the arithmetic mean of all x_i.

$$\bar{x} = \frac{1}{n} \sum_{i=1}^{n} x_i$$

The law of large numbers states that the sample mean $\bar{x}$ converges to the true mean μ as the sample size n increases. In other words, if you are trying to predict something, more data helps. The remainder of this section will explain why.

We will rely on the assumption that the variance of x_i is constant across i. In other words, the variance is $\sigma_{x_i}^2 = \sigma^2$ for all i. The properties of variance asserted by elementary statistics tell us the following about the sample mean, $\bar{x}$.

$$\sigma_{\bar{x}}^2 = \frac{\sigma^2}{n}$$

The standard deviation of x_i is $\sigma = \sqrt{\sigma^2}$. As a result, we can write the standard deviation of $\bar{x}$ as the following.

$$\sigma_{\bar{x}} = \frac{\sigma}{\sqrt{n}}$$

The above equation has a big impact on how we interpret studies, news, events, and many other forms of analysis in our daily lives. For example, the size a confidence interval of a mean can determine whether or not the result of a study is statistically significant. Similarly, the size of the confidence interval of a prediction can determine whether or not the prediction is actionable. When confidence intervals are too wide, the model is not useful because none of its outputs are significant or actionable.

How does one go about shrinking confidence intervals? If your data are independent and identically distributed (i.i.d.) and you have the ability to collect more of it, you can shrink any given confidence interval by 50% by collecting four times as much data.

Strictly statistically speaking, $\bar{x}$ is an *estimator* of μ. The law of large numbers tells us that it is a *good estimator* because it converges to μ with increasing n. Other more advanced estimators in statistics and machine learning follow similar rules regarding convergence. We will go into some detail about which methods provide direct opportunities to shrink confidence intervals via additional data.

2.2.1   Example: Estimating a Sample Mean

Given an estimate of the mean $\bar{x}$, the sample standard deviation $\hat{\sigma}$ is defined as follows.

$$\hat{\sigma}^2 = \frac{1}{n-1} \sum_{i=1}^{n} (x_i - \bar{x})^2$$

Given that n is much larger than 30, the 95% confidence interval for the estimate of the mean is the following, based on the Student's t-distribution.

$$\bar{x} \pm 1.96 \frac{\hat{\sigma}}{\sqrt{n}}$$

As such, the size of the confidence interval is approximately the following.

$$2 * 1.96 \frac{\hat{\sigma}}{\sqrt{n}} \approx 4 \frac{\hat{\sigma}}{\sqrt{n}}$$

Therefore, if your data are i.i.d., have constant variance, and you have the ability to collect more of it, the confidence interval for your estimate of the mean can be shrunk by a factor of $\sqrt{\frac{n'}{n}}$ if you increase the size of your sample from n to n'. See Figure 2.1 for an example.

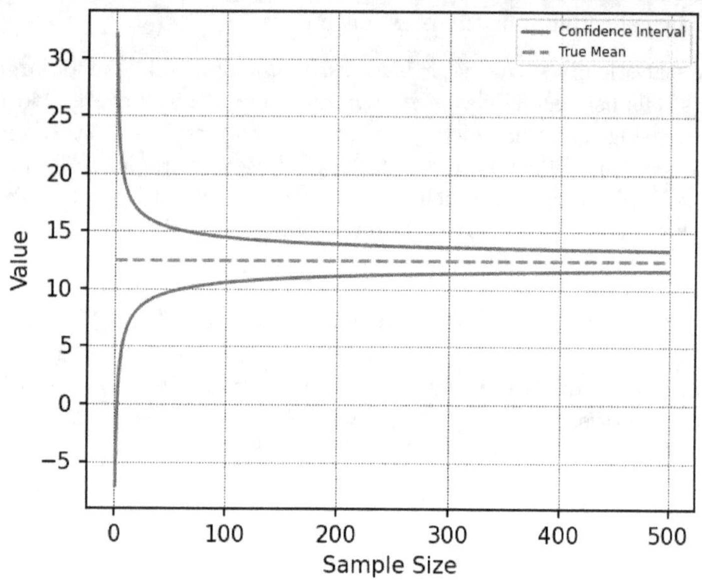

Figure 2.1: Confidence interval for $\bar{x}$ based on n

2.2.2   Example: Simple Linear Regression

A simple linear regression estimates the values of y_i as $\hat{y}_i$ for $i \in 1, ..., n$ as follows, given a set of predictors x_i, where α and β represent fitted parameters.

$$\hat{y}_i = \alpha + \beta x_i$$

The following is a formula for the 95% confidence interval of a prediction for a new value y_k where $k \notin 1, ..., n$, given n is much larger than 30.

$$\hat{y}_k \pm 1.96 * \sqrt{MSE * \left(\frac{1}{n} + \frac{(x_k - \bar{x})^2}{SSD} \right)}$$

Necessarily, the size of the confidence interval is twice the value of the right-hand side of the above expression. Here, the SSD represents the sum of squared deviations of x_i from its sample mean and is calculated as follows.

$$SSD = \sum_{i=1}^{n} (x_i - \bar{x})^2$$

Further, MSE represents the sum of squared errors of the predictions $\hat{y}_i$ from the values they aim to predict, y_i, and is calculated as follows.

$$MSE = \frac{1}{n} \sum_{i=1}^{n} (\hat{y}_i - y_i)^2$$

Putting it all together without endeavoring to understand or prove the above, we can study the effects of increasing the sample size on the size of the confidence interval. We will consider a few scenarios. The size of the 95% confidence interval for $x_k \approx \bar{x}$ is approximately the following, where $RMSE = \sqrt{MSE}$.

$$4 * \frac{RMSE}{\sqrt{n}}$$

When $x_k \approx \bar{x}$, the numerator of the SSD expression becomes zero and the size of the confidence interval takes on the above simple form, which is proportional to $\frac{1}{\sqrt{n}}$.

This looks remarkably similar to the formula for $\sigma_{\bar{x}}$ in the previous discussion about the law of large numbers. If your goal, as a data business executive, is to reduce the size of the confidence intervals for your regression model for some x_k near $\bar{x}$, all you need to do is increase n without increasing MSE. If your data is i.i.d. with constant variance, then this is often very feasible. If you would like to increase the accuracy of your estimates at points far away from $\bar{x}$, then the problem is more complex.

When x_k is far from $\bar{x}$, the error of the estimate is larger due to the effect of the $(x_k - \bar{x})^2$ term in our first equation. This is an intentional feature of linear regression models that penalizes accuracy based on the degree of extrapolation. See Figure 2.2 for an illustration of this concept.

Fortunately, it is not difficult to increase the size of SSD by collecting additional data. The SSD has no denominator or deflationary term, so all that is required is to add additional data in an evenly distributed fashion around $\bar{x}$. In other words, don't just add data at one tail, because it will move $\bar{x}$. Again, if your data are truly i.i.d., then this should not be a problem.

2.2.3   Conclusion

We have shown how the relationship between confidence intervals and sample sizes applies to both estimates of single numbers and estimates generated by statistical models. We have also shown that it applies to both estimates of means and estimates of functional relationships.

An Analysis of Variance (ANOVA) model is a model of averages organized by category. Since the principle applies to both statistical models and to estimates of means, it applies to ANOVA models. Such is the case, and the corresponding formula exists. We will leave it as an exercise to the reader to investigate further.

A similar argument can be made for Generalized Linear Models (GLMs), because they combine the linear predictive estimators of linear regression models with the category-wise mean effects estimators of ANOVA models. A standard formula for the confidence interval of an estimate generated by a GLM model is not well-documented or readily available, but we can be reasonably certain that the

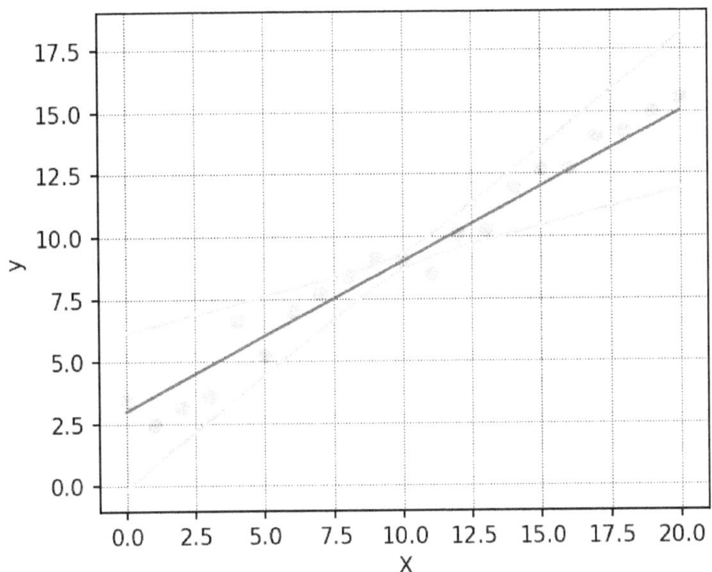

Figure 2.2: Confidence interval for out-of-sample prediction of linear regression

square root principle of uncertainty applies to it. As a stepping stone to understanding confidence intervals for GLMs, readers are encouraged to investigate confidence interval formulae for multiple linear regressions.

2.3   Power of a Statistical Test

The power of a statistical test is the probability of avoiding a type II error, given that the the null hypothesis is false. If we define power as β, then $1 - \beta$ is the probability that you did nothing when you should have made a data-driven decision. In a business context, increasing β decreases the occurrence of missed opportunities. For this discussion, it suffices to say that we want to maximize it.

The statistical power of a test has a relationship with the significance level of a test. As a matter of best practice, statisticians should target a significance level of $\alpha = 0.05$ and a power of $\beta = 0.80$. However, power is rarely measured or targeted in practice.

The following is a general formula for statistical power, given the true value of the test statistic μ_X of a random variable X and a z-score z_α based on a one-sided significance level α. The alternative hypothesis in this formula is that the true value of the test statistic on X is greater than 0.

$$\beta \approx 1 - \Phi\left(z_\alpha - \frac{\mu_X}{\hat{\sigma}_x / \sqrt{n}}\right)$$

In the above formula, Φ is the cumulative normal distribution function and n is assumed to be large enough to satisfy the normality assumption $(n > 30)$ for the sample statistic on X.

Since μ_X cannot be directly measured, practitioners typically simulate the shape of the power curve based on assumed values of μ_X. Further, power curve simulations show that β is monotonically increasing with n. We can analytically verify this based on the shape of the error function $\Phi(\cdot)$. Figure 2.3 shows a simulated power curve for increasing n given some example values for the sample variance and test statistic.

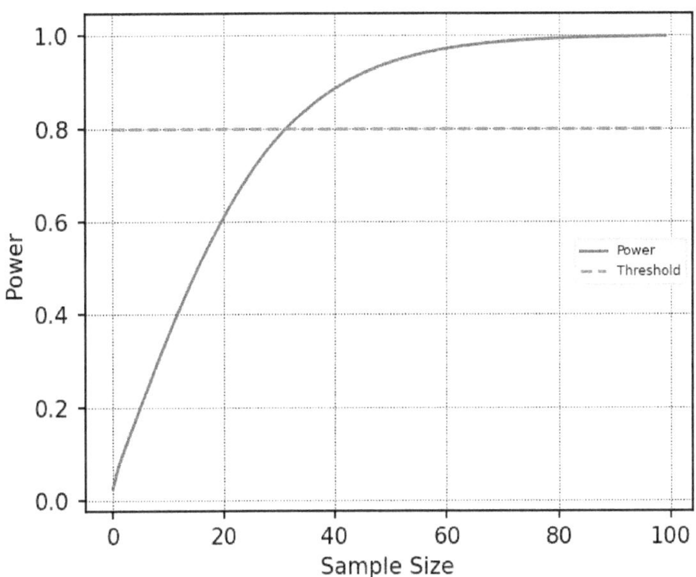

Figure 2.3: Power curve for $z_\alpha = 1.96$, $\mu_X = 1$, and $\hat{\sigma}_x = 2$

How is this formula relevant to a business decision maker? It states that small data sets increase the probability that you will fail to reject null hypothesis. In the business world, the null hypothesis is equivalent to the *status quo*. If you incorrectly accept the status quo, your business will fail to make the necessary changes to survive and grow.

2.4   Translation of Volatility

To start, we assume that asset prices, y_t, follow a Geometric Brownian Motion, which gives us the follow formula inspired by Kerry Back.

The translation of volatility to and from different time scales is one of the most important consequences of the square root rule of uncertainty in applied finance. We start by assuming that asset prices, y_t, follow a Geometric Brownian Motion (GBM), as such, inspired by *A Course in Derivative Securities* by Kerry Back (2005).

$$\frac{dy(t)}{y(t)} = \mu \, dt + \sigma \, dB(t)$$

In the above equation, $B(t)$ is a standard normal Brownian motion and $y(t)$ is a continuous-time process. The use of parentheses indicates it is continuous as opposed to discrete, which is expressed using a subscript.

A Brownian motion has the following three properties.

1. $B(t)$ is continuous along t, with infinite resolution.
2. $dB(t)$ is an i.i.d. process. Every non-overlapping $B(t+k) - B(t)$ is independent for any values of t and k.
3. $B(t+k) - B(t)$ is normally distributed as $\mathcal{N}(0, k)$ for $k \geq 0$.

As a consequence of these properties, $dB(t)$ can be thought of as a random variable distributed as $\mathcal{N}(0, dt)$. The above formulation is useful for analytical calculus, but the relationship to the square root rule becomes clear when analyzing discretized versions of the formula. To discretize the time series, we sample values from it at a regular interval. The process is similar to how we would construct a candlestick chart from real-time stock prices.

See Figure 2.4 for a simulated GBM that highlights the infinite resolution property by iteratively zooming in on the time series.

2.4.1 Variance in a Discretized GBM

We will start by discretizing $y(t)$ to an interval of k, and we will express the result as y_t. Using this expression, we can develop an equation for the return sampled at an interval k, which we will call $r_{t,k}$.

$$r_{t,k} = \frac{\Delta y_t}{y_{t-k}} = \frac{y_t - y_{t-k}}{y_{t-k}} = \mu k + \sigma X_k$$

In the above equation, X_k is a random normal variable distributed as $\mathcal{N}(0, k)$, as suggested by the properties of Brownian motions. The properties of scaled random normal variables tell us that the mean and variance of $r_{t,k}$ are μk and $\sigma^2 k$, respectively. We can express the random variable $r_{t,k}$ as follows.

$$r_{t,k} \sim \mathcal{N}(\mu k, \sigma^2 k)$$

In other words, the variance of $r_{t,k}$ is a function of the variance of the underlying time series σ^2 and the resampling period k.

2.4.2 Translating Volatility of a GBM

We determined in the last section that a stock price following a Geometric Brownian Motion has a variance of returns that is proportional to its underlying volatility and the time span over which the return is measured. This result becomes interesting when we start to think about volatilities measured over different time spans.

In applied finance, volatility is defined as the sample standard deviation of returns on an asset. The term is used everywhere and people reference it colloquially, despite it being a fairly esoteric concept. We will show in this section how to obtain an estimate for the volatility

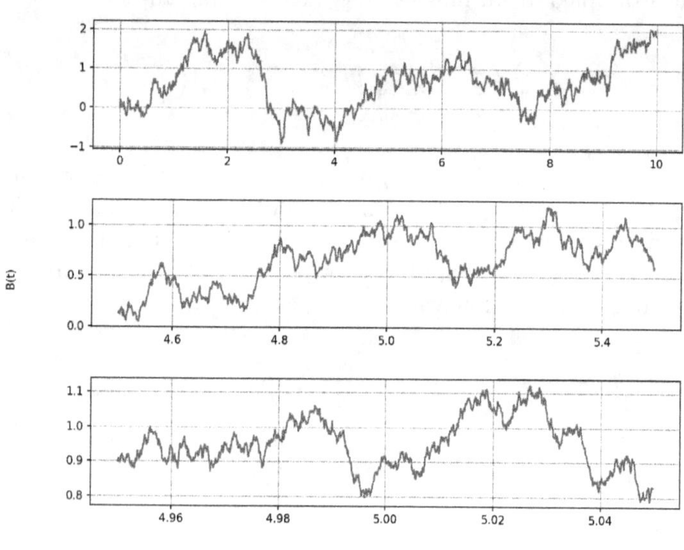

Figure 2.4: A standard normal Brownian motion discretized into different time periods.

on any time span, given an estimate of the volatility measured on a different time span.

Define σ_k as the volatility of y_t measured on $r_{t,k}$. Define σ_m as the volatility of y_t measured on $r_{t,m}$. The volatility of σ_m can be estimated as follows.

$$\hat{\sigma}_m = \sigma_k \sqrt{\frac{m}{k}}$$

In other words, if we have access to daily returns (k is one day), and we want to compute annualized volatility on an asset (m is one year), we multiply our measured daily volatility σ_k by the square root of the length of a year over the length of a day. In practice, we typically consider there to be 252 trading days in a year, so we multiply by $\sqrt{\frac{252}{1}} = \sqrt{252} \approx 15.8$. This often results in better and more sensitive estimates of annualized volatility than we could otherwise get using yearly returns, and it is a standard estimation method in finance.

Many types of assets can be shown to exhibit properties of Geometric Brownian Motions, and this estimation method can be show to be very stable. It works for translating volatilities both up and down time scales, which makes it a very useful mathematical tool to have in your arsenal. For example, what if you need to compare the annualized volatility of one asset to another type of asset for which you only have weekly, biweekly, or monthly returns? You would reference this formula and compute the translation factor $\sqrt{m/k}$. There is not often an abundance of data in finance, so you will often find yourself in such situations.

In my business, I have programmed this relationship into all of our volatility calculations so that our numbers are annualized by default. Some creative computer science with date-aware data structures can allow you to estimate the translation factor on the fly, without making any assumptions about the shape of the data or the resampling period.

Chapter 3

Surviving on Beta

Suppose that an investment analyst has developed an investment strategy, and he wants to start an investment fund based on his strategy. The strategy has seemingly good historical performance according to some risk-return metrics, including the Sharpe Ratio.

The analyst's next step in starting his fund is to go out and raise outside capital for his fund. To raise outside capital, he will meet with numerous investors and pitch his strategy to each of them. Some of his investors will be more experienced than others, and some of them will be more scrutinous than others. As long as he secures enough investment, he will have enough capital to launch his fund.

If the analyst provides consistent outperforming returns to his investors, he will be rewarded and his fund will grow. If he underperforms or loses money, he risks having his investors pull their capital. If enough investors pull their capital, the fund will have to close, because it will not earn enough fees to stay open.

In this chapter, we will analyze the relationship between alpha, beta, CAGR, and the Sharpe Ratio to understand why so many investment funds open and close within a given business cycle. We will also analyze the business opportunity and the business risk of running a high-beta strategy in a bull market.

3.1 Performance Metrics

This section will define some performance metrics for the purposes of our discussion. Performance metrics defined here, in a financial reporting and strategy comparison context, will differ somewhat from performance metrics defined in other mathematical arguments within this book.

The equity curve E_t for $t \in 1, ..., T$ is the sum of all cash and portfolio holdings of the firm at each time t. We define E_0 as the starting capital of the firm. For this discussion, t will represent yearly increments. The Compounded Annual Growth Rate (CAGR) of E_t is the annualized total return. This value represents the equivalent yearly compounded interest rate earned by the firm through its investing activities. We will denote the CAGR as r_a.

$$r_a = \left(\frac{E_T}{E_0} \right)^{\frac{1}{T}} - 1$$

The Sharpe Ratio is the CAGR, less the annualized benchmark return r_b, divided by the volatility of returns on E_t. We will denote the Sharpe Ratio as ϕ.

$$\phi = \frac{r_a - r_b}{\sigma_r}$$

The alpha and beta (α and β) of a portfolio are the coefficients of the following regression equation, where r_t is the annual return on E_t and q_t is the annual return on a benchmark index.

$$r_t = \alpha + \beta q_t + \epsilon$$

See Figure 3.1 for an example of a high-alpha portfolio and a high-beta portfolio, per the above equation. Alpha is an estimate of investment management skill, and beta is the scaled correlation between the benchmark returns and the portfolio returns.

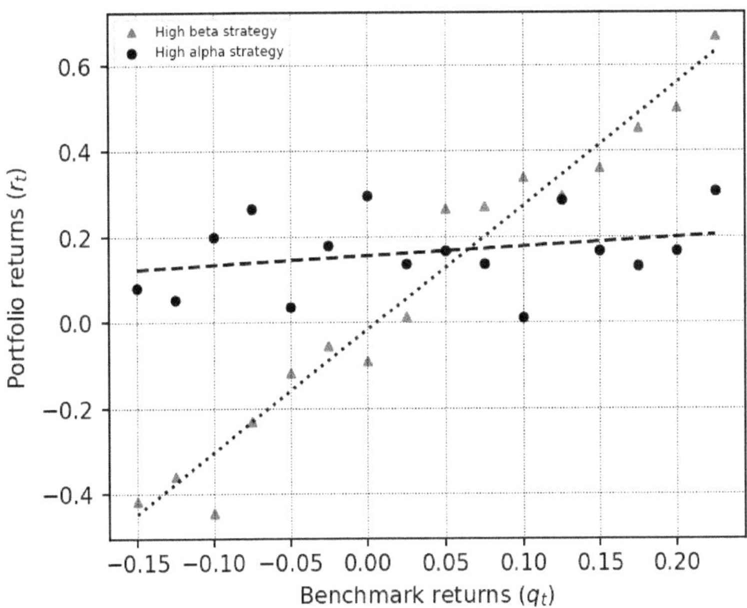

Figure 3.1: Sample high alpha and high beta portfolios

We will take advantage of the following relationship between E_t and r_t in order to explore relationships between the above-listed performance metrics.

$$E_t = E_0 \prod_{i=1}^{t}(1 + r_i)$$

The benchmarks in both of the above equations are typically the S&P 500 in a stock-picking context. Our core argument will be that non-zero alpha is difficult to generate, but the beta and Sharpe Ratio can be easily manipulated.

3.2   Types of Investment Strategies

The following are some useful properties of the above-listed performance metrics.

1. $\phi = 0$, $\alpha = 0$, and $\beta = 1$ for the benchmark portfolio.
2. $\alpha = 0$ and $\beta = \beta_0$ for a benchmark portfolio levered β_0 times.

In this section, we will attempt to express ϕ in terms of α and β under various sets of assumptions in order to learn about how different types of strategies are represented by different performance metrics.

3.2.1   Leveraged Benchmark Strategy

If the investor simply invests in the benchmark, he will achieve $\phi = 0$, $\alpha = 0$, and $\beta = 1$, arising from the fact that $r_t = q_t$ in this scenario.

If the investor uses a levered account to invest in the benchmark, we will see some interesting changes in the performance metrics. Assume that the leverage multiple is β_0, and the investor achieves yearly returns of $r_t = \beta_0 q_t$. In this scenario, we have the following regression equation to solve for α and β.

$$\beta_0 q_t = \alpha + \beta q_t + \epsilon$$

It can be shown that the above regression equation is solved by $\alpha = 0$ and $\beta = \beta_0$ for any possible values of q_t.

In order to solve for ϕ, we need to study how leverage affects the CAGR, r_{a,β_0}, in terms of the above. We start with the following.

$$E_{T,\beta_0} = E_0 \prod_{t=1}^{T}(1 + \beta_0 q_t)$$

$$r_{a,\beta_0} = \left(\frac{E_{T,\beta_0}}{E_0}\right)^{\frac{1}{T}} - 1$$

It can be shown empirically that r_{a,β_0} is very close to $\beta_0 * r_a$ for strictly positives values of q_t, so we will proceed under the assumption that $r_{a,\beta_0} = \beta_0 * r_a$. This is not an unrealistic assumption, since many performance reports from investment funds contain strictly positive yearly returns.

With this, we can express the Sharpe Ratio in terms of the leveraged portfolio, by substituting in $\beta_0 * r_b$ for r_a.

$$\phi = \frac{r_b(\beta_0 - 1)}{\sigma_r}$$

In other words, the Sharpe Ratio of a levered benchmark portfolio is proportional to one less than the leverage multiple. Say, for example, that the S&P 500 had a CAGR of 5% and an annualized volatility of 15%. An analyst could achieve a Sharpe Ratio of 3 by holding the benchmark at a leverage multiple of 10 on flat and positive years. Of course, this is unrealistic in practice, but worse sins have been committed in strategy simulations. As part of this simulation, the analyst would have reported a CAGR of 50%.

This discussion is intended to make investors cautious of various ways that Sharpe Ratio and CAGR can be manipulated in historical performance reports and simulations. Of course, the easiest way to poke a hole in a leveraged benchmark portfolio is inquire about the alpha and beta, which would be $\alpha = 0$ and $\beta = 10$ in the above example.

Further, this discussion is more than a fun thought experiment. There are a large number of investment funds in the market today that closely resemble leveraged benchmark strategies. For example, a leveraged portfolio of a diverse set of randomly selected small-cap stocks would be high-beta and zero-alpha. If a strategy like this possesses no intrinsic informational advantage, then it is no different from a leveraged benchmark strategy.

3.2.2   An Ideal Actively Managed Strategy

The ideal actively managed strategy is completely uncorrelated to the market, giving it $\beta = 0$, but it also outperforms the market consistently, giving it $\alpha > 0$. This section will describe such a strategy in concrete but realistic terms, then express its Sharpe Ratio and CAGR in terms of its alpha and beta.

Suppose that every year the strategy returns either a good return or a bad return. It returns a good return with probability p and a bad return with probability $1 - p$. Every good return is always the same, $r^+ = \alpha_0 + \gamma$, and every bad return is always the same, $r^- = \alpha_0 - \gamma$, where $\gamma > 0$. The yearly returns r_t can be modeled as a scaled and translated Bernoulli variable $X \sim B(p)$ where $X \in \{0, 1\}$. We can express the yearly returns as the following random variable.

$$r_t \sim \alpha_0 + \gamma(2X - 1)$$

See Figure 3.2 for a schematic of our toy portfolio parameters r_t. Per the definition of a Bernoulli random variable, the mean r_t is as follows.

$$\mu_r = \alpha_0 + \gamma(2p - 1)$$

We should note that α_0 is just a parameter in this equation, not the alpha of the portfolio. The portfolio alpha α is measured via a linear regression. Using the properties of linear regression, it can be shown that $\mu_r = \alpha$. In other words, α is the measured alpha on a portfolio parameterized by α_0, γ, and p.

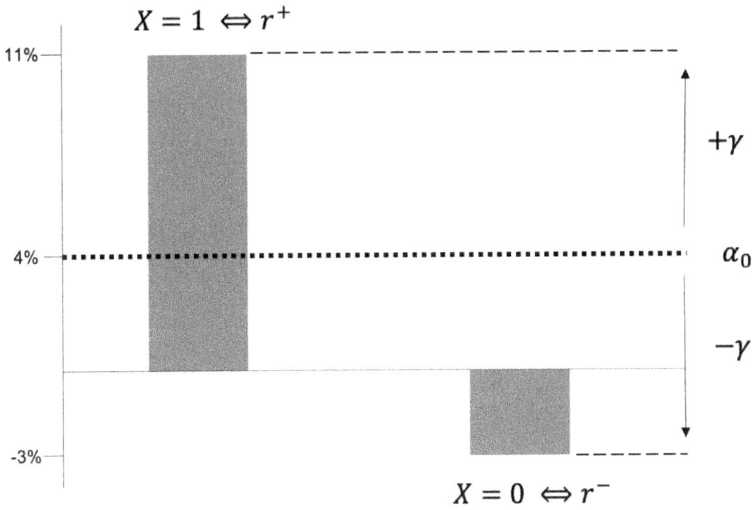

Figure 3.2: Toy portfolio parameters

It should also be noted here that $\mu_r = \alpha = \alpha_0$ for $p = \frac{1}{2}$. Further, per the definition of a Bernoulli random variable, we can express the standard deviation of r_t as follows.

$$\sigma_r = 2\gamma\sqrt{p(1-p)}$$

It should be noted here that $\sigma_r = \gamma$ for $p = \frac{1}{2}$ and $\sigma_r \approx \gamma/2$ for $p = \frac{14}{15}$.

As we can see in the equation for σ_r, the volatility of the portfolio only depends on γ and p. The investment manager would prefer to have $\gamma = 0$, which would result in a perfectly uniform return series of $r_t = \alpha_0$, but this is unrealistic. He must contend with some uncertainty in his otherwise very consistent strategy, and the uncertainty coefficient γ affects the volatility of his portfolio.

To measure the Sharpe Ratio, we need to express r_a in terms of α and β. For analytical simplicity, we will use the arithmetic mean of returns rather than the CAGR (the geometric mean) for r_a, which allows us to set r_a equal to μ_r. With this, we have the following expanded formula for the Sharpe Ratio.

$$\phi = \frac{\alpha_0 + \gamma(2p-1) - r_b}{2\gamma\sqrt{p(1-p)}}$$

We can start to learn more about how different versions of the strategy work by exploring relationships between the uncertainty coefficient γ, the midpoint of the range of returns α_0, and the frequency of good returns p.

For example, if we set $p = 0.5$, we can reduce the expression considerably. This expresses the Sharpe Ratio of a completely uncorrelated portfolio that earns earns an annual return of r^+ or r^- each year according to a coin flip.

$$\phi = \frac{\alpha_0 - r_b}{\gamma} = \frac{\alpha - r_b}{\gamma}$$

In other words, the coin flip portfolio will earn an extra unit of Sharpe Ratio each time α exceeds r_b by γ. For a benchmark return of 5% and an uncertainty coefficient of 10%, the mean outperformance would need to be 35% to achieve a Sharpe Ratio of 3. In this example, r^+ and r^- would be 45% and 25%, respectively. This is aspirational even for a high-return discretionary equities fund. It also highlights a key drawback of the Sharpe Ratio, in practice. One might argue that the variations within highly outperforming returns should not be penalized by the denominator as they are in this example. Nonetheless, we include it for sake of consistency and comparison.

We will now look at another portfolio that earns r^+ with a probability of $p = \frac{14}{15}$. We will use the definitions $\sqrt{p(1-p)} = \frac{1}{4}$ and $(4p-2) = \frac{26}{15} = \eta$ for this portfolio.

$$\phi = \frac{2(\alpha_0 - r_b)}{\gamma} + \eta$$

It is worth pointing out that the alpha on the portfolio would be the following.

$$\alpha = \alpha_0 + \gamma\frac{\eta}{2}$$

The above expressions tell us that this portfolio would have a Sharpe Ratio of $\phi = \eta = 1.73$ if the midpoint of return distribution was equal to the benchmark, $\alpha_0 = r_b$. In other words, if an investment strategy outperforms the benchmark by any percentage γ for every 14 of 15 years, it will have a Sharpe Ratio of $\eta = 1.73$ regardless of the size of γ.

If the strategy has $\alpha_0 > r_b$, the Sharpe Ratio will increase by $\frac{2}{\gamma}$ for every unit increase in α_0. For example, if a version of this strategy with a γ value of 10% wanted to increase its Sharpe Ratio by 1, it would have to increase α_0 by 5%, which is a very difficult task. In order for this strategy to achieve a Sharpe Ratio of 3 against the S&P 500 ($r_b = 5\%$), it would need to achieve an α_0 of 11.3%, which would imply a measured α of 20%. This is extremely difficult.

If nothing else, this discussion has shows that the Sharpe Ratio can be either very punishing or very forgiving for different types of strategies. It provides a helpful yardstick for comparing strategies of similar character, but it can be very misleading when used to compare strategies that rely on different investment styles.

In practice, quantitative investment analysts use more complex measurements than the Sharpe Ratio for evaluating portfolio performance and selecting an optimal investment strategy. Almost always, there exists a unique performance metric that appropriately optimizes for the desired risk-return profile.

3.3 Conclusion

This chapter discussed how high-beta zero-alpha investment funds are able to start and temporarily thrive by manipulating common risk-adjusted return metrics to bury intrinsic risk. We also discussed how difficult it can be to achieve a high Sharpe Ratio on zero-beta strategies, which may provide some evidence as to why some of the top-performing discretionary equities funds in the world do not advertise Sharpe Ratios.

Chapter 4

Better Performance Metrics

We have spent two chapters so far in this book conducting analytical experiments on Sharpe Ratios to try to learn about risk-adjusted return. In some cases, we have extrapolated insights about risk from derivations that rely on the Sharpe Ratio. In other cases, we have exploited portfolio construction schemes to create intentionally misleading Sharpe Ratios.

This chapter will explore better performance metrics that ought to be considered when designing a trading strategy. We will explore some of their desirable mathematical properties, and hopefully provide some inspiration as to how to engineer your own performance metric that prioritizes your desired investment performance.

4.1   Why Sharpe is Popular

The Sharpe Ratio is not a good objective function for your trading strategy. It is used in applied finance for two reasons.

1. Most people know how to interpret it.
2. It is easy to do math with.

Most people know how to interpret the Sharpe Ratio in the sense that most sophisticated investors are familiar with elementary statistics, and they know that the Sharpe Ratio ought to be interpreted like a z-score.

The Sharpe Ratio has proliferated so intensely in academic literature because it is mathematically very simple. It draws on a lot of mathematical identities from classical statistics, which means it can be manipulated easily in mathematical arguments to attempt to make specific points about the nature of risk-adjusted returns. Inevitably, many of these assertions about risk-adjusted returns are not really about risk-adjusted returns. Rather, they are about risk-adjusted returns as they are measured by the Sharpe Ratio.

It is important to remember that the Sharpe Ratio is only an estimate of risk-adjusted return. Further, it is far from a perfect measure. This chapter will analyze a number of alternative and superior metrics that ought to be used in practice. Readers will see that these metrics are necessarily more complex, more specific, and more discretized. If one were to attempt to derive some of the arguments from the first or third chapters of this book using these metrics, the resulting math would be quite messy and uninterpretable.

4.2   Alternative Metrics

This section will define a number of alternative risk-return metrics. The following section will use these definitions to perform a thorough comparison.

4.2.1   Sortino Ratio

The Sortino Ratio is defined as follows, where r_a is the annualized portfolio return, r_b is the annualized benchmark return, and σ_d is the downside deviation of returns, r_t.

$$\text{Sortino Ratio} = \frac{r_a - r_b}{\sigma_d}$$

We measure σ_d as follows. The formula is very similar to the formulas for measuring volatility and sample standard deviation. In statistical language, the formula for σ_d of the Sortino Ratio is the square root of the negative semi-variance of r_t, assuming r_b is the mean of r_t.

$$\sigma_d^2 = \frac{1}{T^-} \sum_{t=1}^{T} \max[r_b - r_t, 0]^2$$

In the above formula, T^- represents the number of returns r_t that were below r_b.

Notice that the summand is zero for any $r_t \geq r_b$. In other words, any returns in excess of r_b do not inflate the denominator, which is the measurement of risk. The Sortino Ratio addresses one of the most obvious complaints about the Sharpe Ratio. The denominator of the Sharpe Ratio, due to the way volatility is calculated, penalizes large upward swings in the value of the portfolio. The denominator of the Sortino Ratio, by contrast, only penalizes downward swings.

4.2.2 Maximum Drawdown Ratios

The maximum drawdown of an equity curve E_t is as follows for $t \in 1, ..., T$ and $i \in 1, ..., T - t$.

$$d = \max[f(E_t, E_{t+i})]$$

In the above formula, $f(x, y)$ is a distance function that describes how much y has fallen down from x. Common choices for f are the log drawdown $\log(x) - \log(y)$ and the percentage drawdown $1 - \frac{y}{x}$.

We will prefer the log max drawdown ratio, which is as follows, given the total log return $r = \log(E_T) - \log(E_0)$.

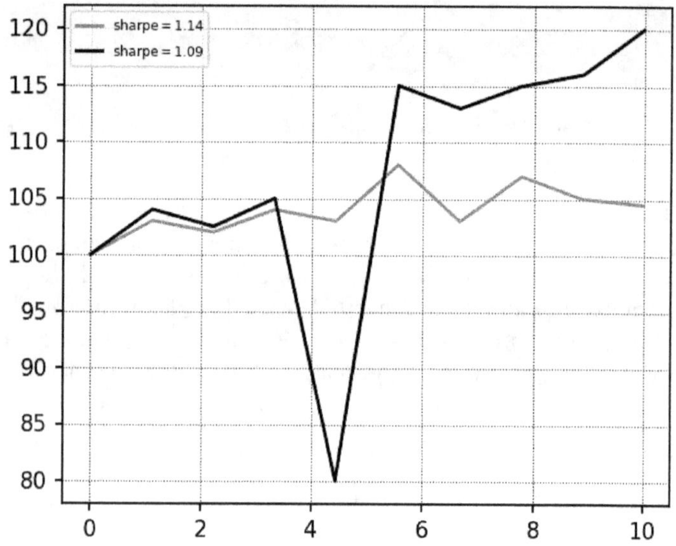

Figure 4.1: The denominator of the Sharpe Ratio causes it to prefer the stable portfoilo with mediocre gains.

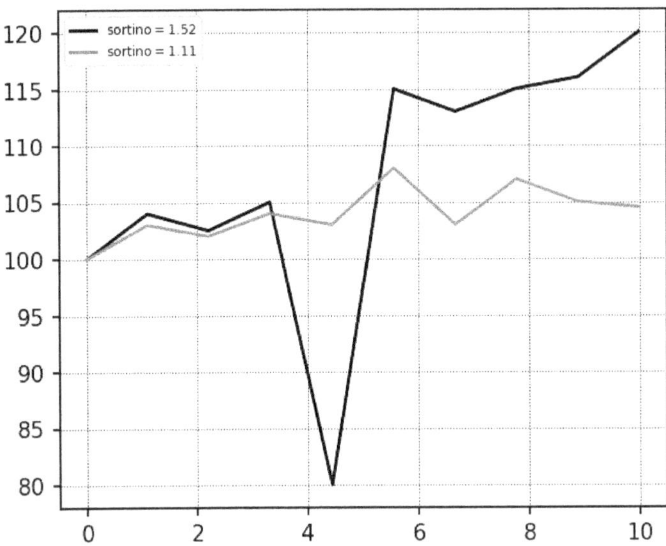

Figure 4.2: The Sortino Ratio prefers the portfolio that stages a strong but sudden recovery.

$$\text{Log Max Drawdown Ratio} = r - d$$

If we define $t = j$ as the peak and $t = k$ as the trough of the drawdown identified by d, we can rewrite the formula in the following interesting way.

$$\text{Log Max Drawdown Ratio} = \log\left(E_T\right) - \log\left(E_0\right) - \left(\log\left(E_j\right) - \log\left(E_k\right)\right)$$

Generalizations of this equation exist where the right-hand side of the expression is not just the size of the largest drawdown, but the mean of the top-n distinct drawdown paths that occurred from $t \in 1, ..., T$.

4.2.3   Drawdown-as-variance Ratios

Drawdown-as-variance ratios are a mathematical combination of the Sortino Ratio and the maximum drawdown ratio. These ratios are similar to value-at-risk (VaR) ratios, but are more robust. For example, the Burke Ratio is as follows.

$$\text{Burke Ratio} = \frac{r_a - r_b}{\sigma_k}$$

In the above equation, σ_k is defined as the sample standard deviation of the top k portfolio drawdowns. It can be expressed as follows, where D_j is the size of the j-th largest drawdown.

$$\sigma_k^2 = \frac{1}{k} \sum_{j=1}^{k} D_j^2$$

When computing this value, the analyst must ensure that drawdowns are measured over distinct timespans.

4.2.4 Alpha and Beta

We discussed alpha and beta in Chapter 3 when comparing them to the Sharpe Ratio. For completeness, we will include them here. See Chapter 3 for more detail. In practice, α and β are measured against the log returns of the portfolio r_t, and the log returns of the benchmark q_t, measured on a monthly or yearly basis. The coefficients are discovered by fitting the following regression equation.

$$r_t = \alpha + \beta q_t + \epsilon$$

In practice, it is important to use log returns, because linear regressions are assumed to operate on normally distributed error terms. For explanation and discussion as to why this is, see Chris Conlan's Algorithmic Trading with Python (2020).

4.2.5 Arbitrary Cost Functions

Sometimes, we want to know if a trading strategy is capable of a specific type of performance. We might tweak the money-management parameters iteratively to see if we can achieve a desired result. This might be considered backtest overfitting, but it can be useful nonetheless to learn about the mathematical boundaries of your trading strategy.

For example, analyst might break up the returns into monthly increments and try to maximize the following objective function.

$$\sum_{t=1}^{T} \begin{cases} 0.2 * (r_t - r_b) & r_t > r_b \\ -3 * (r_b - r_t) & r_t \leq r_b \end{cases}$$

While this function seems incredibly arbitrary, it may reveal something interesting about the strategy. In other words, you may want to optimize the strategy against this cost function, then observe the values of

CAGR, Sharpe, Sortino, and Burke upon its completion. The end result may be a happy medium between many disagreeing performance metrics.

For example, if below-benchmark returns are penalized so heavily, will it be capable of beating the benchmark all the time? If it is not capable of beating the benchmark all the time, how much of the upside will it have to sacrifice to minimize underperforming years? In many ways, the above equation reflects the cost function against which real clients will evaluate investment funds. They may shrug in response to overperforming years, and they likely raise complaints in underperforming years.

Chapter 5

Better Base Estimators

Base estimators are the fundamental building block of statistical models and machine learning algorithms. This chapter will make some assertions about the best base estimators, and consequently the best models, to use in a financial context.

Throughout this chapter, we will assume that a typical set of financial data has the following properties.

- A low signal-to-noise ratio.
- Some features are useful, some of the time.
- Not all features are useful.
- No features are useful all of the time.
- The usefulness of one feature depends on the state of another feature.
- Interaction effects are necessary to develop an effective model.

We will define some base estimators and some toy data sets and explore the mathematical relationships between each to make some generalized conclusions about the best types of models for financial data sets. This chapter will offer brief mathematical definitions of different types of base estimators, but will assume the reader has some background with machine learning models.

5.1 Types of Base Estimators

In this chapter, we will look at a few key base estimators.

5.1.1 Vanilla Linear Terms

Vanilla linear terms are those used in vanilla linear regressions of the following form.

$$y_i = \alpha + \beta_1 x_{i,1} + \beta_2 x_{i,2} + ... + \beta_m x_{i,m} + \epsilon$$

These base estimators are capable of learning linear relationships and incapable of learning non-linear relationships. The maximum number of parameters in a model is $m + 1$.

5.1.2 Linear Interaction Terms

Linear interaction terms are typically used in generalized linear regressions. Interactions are typically described in terms of the product of two or more features. For example, a model with complete one-way and two-way interactions would look like the following, where $\gamma_{j,k}$ represents the two-way interaction coefficient between features j and k.

$$y_i = \alpha + \sum_{j=1}^{m} \beta_j x_{i,j} + \sum_{j=1}^{m} \sum_{k>j} \gamma_{j,k} x_{i,j} x_{i,k}$$

These base estimators have the capability of learning non-linear relationships of order v for a fully v-way general linear regression. They cannot learn arbitrarily non-linear relationships, given that y_i relies solely on the sum of scaled products of the features.

The maximum number of two-way interaction parameters is $\dfrac{m(m-1)}{2}$. Broadly, the maximum number of v-way interaction parameters is $\binom{m}{v}$.

5.1.3 Neural Perceptions

Perceptions are the building blocks of neural networks. Given a neuron in a neural network accepts a vector of inputs x, parameterized by a vector of weights w and a bias b, the output of the neuron has the following form, for some activation function f.

$$f(x^\top w + b)$$

In this chapter, we will assume f is a binary step activation function with the following form.

$$f(x) = \begin{cases} 0 & x < 0 \\ 1 & x \geq 0 \end{cases}$$

It can be shown that chaining these neurons together in a feedforward network can allow a sufficiently deep network to learn any functional form. The number of parameters required to learn a given functional form can be substantial, given that each node has $m + 1$ parameters for m input connections.

5.1.4 Node Splits

The final base estimator we will look at is the core component of decision trees. A node split is simply a binary activation function of the following form, where b is a breakpoint parameter and $c \in \{0, 1\}$ is a direction parameter.

$$f(x) = \begin{cases} 1 - c & x < b \\ c & x \geq b \end{cases}$$

Within a tree of many nodes, a zero causes the sample to descend the left of the tree, and a one causes the sample to descend the right of the tree. If the node is a leaf node, meaning it is the last node in a tree, then the output of the activation function is the output of the model.

Every node split operates on a single scalar value of the data set. A decision tree comprised of many node splits will intelligently choose the column on which to split for every node. First, it chooses which feature j to split the data on. Then, it chooses the breakpoint b on which to split. Finally, it chooses the direction of the split c, where c is a method of manipulating the order of comparison between x and b. In other words, each node of the tree has three parameters.

It can be shown that a composition of node splits in a sufficiently deep decision tree can learn any functional form.

5.2 Types of Data

This section will define various toy data sets and explore how our base estimators interact with them.

5.2.1 Classic XOR Problem

The XOR problem is a classic example in machine learning literature that attempts to show how models can learn to solve highly non-linear problems. In this problem, the training data set consists of an $n \times 2$ matrix of features X and an $n \times 1$ vector of labels y. In the training data, $y_i = 0$ whenever the corresponding $x_{i,1}$ and $x_{i,2}$ are both zero or both one. Otherwise, $y_i = 1$. An example might look like the following.

$$X = \begin{bmatrix} 0 & 0 \\ 1 & 0 \\ 0 & 1 \\ 1 & 1 \end{bmatrix} \qquad y = \begin{bmatrix} 0 \\ 1 \\ 1 \\ 0 \end{bmatrix}$$

This data set can be used to easily learn about the capabilities of a model. If a model can solve the data set, then it is capable of learning at least some non-linear relationships.

5.2.2 Generalized XOR Problem

Suppose we have an $n \times m$ feature matrix X and an $n \times 1$ label vector y. In this training data, $y_i = 1$ whenever $\sum_{j=1}^{m} X_{i,j} = k$, otherwise $y_i = 0$. An example with $m = 3$ and $k = 2$ might look like the following.

$$
X = \begin{bmatrix} 0 & 0 & 0 \\ 1 & 0 & 0 \\ 0 & 1 & 0 \\ 0 & 0 & 1 \\ 1 & 1 & 0 \\ 1 & 0 & 1 \\ 0 & 1 & 1 \\ 1 & 1 & 1 \end{bmatrix} \qquad y = \begin{bmatrix} 0 \\ 0 \\ 0 \\ 0 \\ 1 \\ 1 \\ 1 \\ 0 \end{bmatrix}
$$

The above sample data set is not characteristically financial. Rather, it is characteristically natural. In other words, a researcher is more likely to see this pattern in nature than in finance, because the structure of the data implies that each column has a distinct and intrinsic effect on the output. In finance, a researcher would be likely to see much more noise, and any single feature may not remain predictive for a significant stretch of time.

5.2.3 Generalized XOR with Noise and Substitution

This problem is a modification of the above. For every row i in the matrix X there will be a number of noisy features m^- and a number of useful features m^+, where $m = m^+ + m^-$. The set of useful features J_i^+ and the set of noisy features J_i^- changes row-by-row. The label y_i only depends on the sum of features in J_i^+.

$$
y_i = \mathbb{1}\left[\left(\sum_{j \in J_i^+} X_{i,j} \right) \equiv k \right]
$$

Additionally, we define $k < m^+$, so that there is always some capability of discovering the label amid the noisy data. In other words, we are solving the same XOR problem in the presence of a lot of noise. An example might look like the following for $m = 6$, $m^+ = 3$, and $k = 2$, where blank spaces are noise.

$$X = \begin{bmatrix} 0 & & 0 & & & 0 \\ 1 & & 0 & 0 & & \\ & & 0 & 1 & 0 & \\ & 0 & & & 0 & 1 \\ 1 & & 1 & 0 & & \\ & 1 & & 0 & & 1 \\ 0 & & 1 & 1 & & \\ & 1 & & 1 & 1 & \end{bmatrix} \qquad y = \begin{bmatrix} 0 \\ 0 \\ 0 \\ 0 \\ 1 \\ 1 \\ 1 \\ 0 \end{bmatrix}$$

In this chapter, we will assume that the noise is randomly distributed between 0 and 1 according to a uniform distribution. We will proceed to analytically solve each of the toy data sets with each base estimator in order to learn about model performance and capabilities in a financial data context.

5.3 Applying the Base Estimators

For each toy data set, we will attempt to analytically or argumentatively solve for the base estimator or a composition of base estimators in the hopes of learning about model selection.

5.3.1 Solving the Classic XOR Problem

The XOR problem provides a simple framework for determining which models are capable of solving non-linear problems.

5.3.1.1 Vanilla Linear Terms

A vanilla linear estimator cannot solve the classic XOR problem satisfactorily. Solving for the following equation to minimize the error term yields an unhelpful result.

$$y_i = \alpha + \beta_1 x_{i,1} + \beta_2 x_{i,2} + \epsilon_i$$

In matrix notation, we would attempt to minimize $\|\epsilon\|$ within the following equation.

$$\begin{bmatrix} 1 & 0 & 0 \\ 1 & 1 & 0 \\ 1 & 0 & 1 \\ 1 & 1 & 1 \end{bmatrix} \begin{bmatrix} \alpha \\ \beta_1 \\ \beta_2 \end{bmatrix} + \begin{bmatrix} \epsilon_1 \\ \epsilon_2 \\ \epsilon_3 \\ \epsilon_4 \end{bmatrix} = \begin{bmatrix} 0 \\ 1 \\ 1 \\ 0 \end{bmatrix}$$

The resultant optimal parameters and error terms are as follows.

$$\begin{bmatrix} \alpha \\ \beta_1 \\ \beta_2 \end{bmatrix} = \begin{bmatrix} 0.5 \\ 0 \\ 0 \end{bmatrix} \qquad \begin{bmatrix} \epsilon_1 \\ \epsilon_2 \\ \epsilon_3 \\ \epsilon_4 \end{bmatrix} = \begin{bmatrix} -0.5 \\ 0.5 \\ 0.5 \\ -0.5 \end{bmatrix}$$

In other words, the vanilla linear regression does not perform better than the sample mean of the label vector $\bar{y} = \frac{1}{2}$ as an estimator. All of the linear coefficients serve best as zeros. As this is the simplest case, vanilla linear terms will not be able to solve any of the toy data sets covered in this chapter.

5.3.1.2 Linear Interaction Terms

With linear interaction terms, we can attempt to solve the following, where the only difference from the prior formula is the addition of a γ coefficient and a sole interaction term.

$$y_i = \alpha + \beta_1 x_{i,1} + \beta_2 x_{i,2} + \gamma_{1,2} x_{i,1} x_{i,2} + \epsilon_i$$

We can attempt to minimize $||\epsilon||$ in the following matrix equation.

$$\begin{bmatrix} 1 & 0 & 0 & 0 \\ 1 & 1 & 0 & 0 \\ 1 & 0 & 1 & 0 \\ 1 & 1 & 1 & 1 \end{bmatrix} \begin{bmatrix} \alpha \\ \beta_1 \\ \beta_2 \\ \gamma_{1,2} \end{bmatrix} + \begin{bmatrix} \epsilon_1 \\ \epsilon_2 \\ \epsilon_3 \\ \epsilon_4 \end{bmatrix} = \begin{bmatrix} 0 \\ 1 \\ 1 \\ 0 \end{bmatrix}$$

The resultant optimal parameters and error terms are as follows.

$$\begin{bmatrix} \alpha \\ \beta_1 \\ \beta_2 \\ \gamma_{1,2} \end{bmatrix} = \begin{bmatrix} 0 \\ 1 \\ 1 \\ -2 \end{bmatrix} \qquad \begin{bmatrix} \epsilon_1 \\ \epsilon_2 \\ \epsilon_3 \\ \epsilon_4 \end{bmatrix} = \begin{bmatrix} 0 \\ 0 \\ 0 \\ 0 \end{bmatrix}$$

In the above solution, $||\epsilon||$ has been minimized to zero. Thus, we have proven that linear interaction terms are able to learn non-linear relationships within the training data. In this case, it has done so with 4 parameters.

5.3.1.3 Neural Perceptrons

A feedforward neural network with one hidden layer is able to solve the classic XOR problem in the following way.

The XOR problem can be decomposed into the following Boolean function, expressed in pseudo-code, where zero and one represent **False** and **True**, respectively.

```
y = (x1 or x2) and (not (x1 and x2))
```

Decomposing further we see that there are three distinct Boolean functions to model.

```
y = (
    (x1 or x2)          # The OR gate
    and                 # The AND gate
    (not (x1 and x2))   # The NOT-AND gate
)
```

A neural network can mimic these logical operators in the structure described by Figure 5.1. For each node, we can define the weights, w_1 and w_2, and the bias b, needed to configure the network.

Node	w_1	w_2	b
OR	+1	+1	-1
NOT-AND	-1	-1	+1
AND	+1	+1	-2

Table 5.1: Neural network parameters to solve XOR

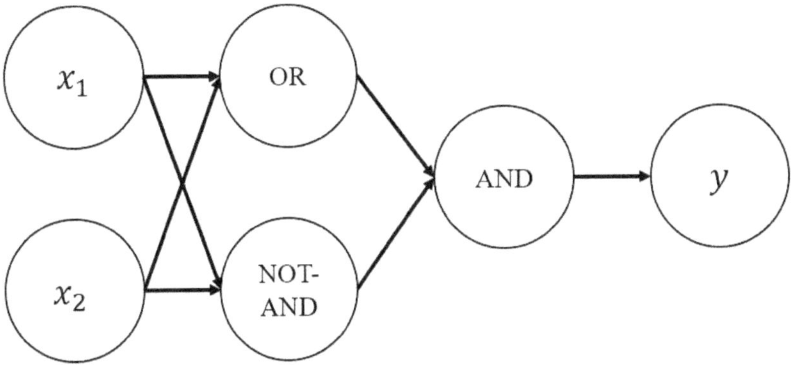

Figure 5.1: The ideal neural network for solving XOR

The network solves the XOR problem in the following way, given the binary step activation function $\mathbb{1}[(x^\top w + b) \geq 0]$.

x_1	x_2	OR	NOT-AND	AND	y
0	0	0	1	0	0
1	0	1	1	1	1
0	1	1	1	1	1
1	1	1	0	0	0

Table 5.2: Neural network calculations to solve XOR

In this solution, there are 9 parameters to the neural network, three for each node. Given m features in the feature matrix X, a feedforward network of this type with one hidden layer will have $m^2 + 2m + 1$ parameters.

5.3.1.4 Node Splits

A decision tree composed of node splits can solve the XOR problem in the following simple way. In theory, the very discretized and non-linear nature of the XOR problem would make it the perfect candidate for a decision tree.

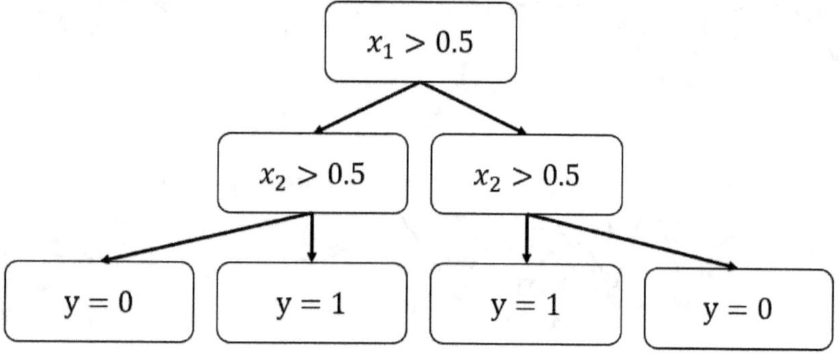

Figure 5.2: The ideal decision tree for solving XOR

This decision tree requires 9 parameters. At each node, the decision tree must decide which feature to use, j, the breakpoint, b, and the direction of the split. As such, the number of parameters in the decision tree is based on the complexity of the function to be solved rather than the configuration of the model.

5.3.2 Solving the Generalized XOR Problem

We will reveal ahead of time that the same set of base estimators that were able to solve the classic XOR problem in the last section are capable of solving the generalized XOR problem. It is not of particular interest how they solve the problem, but it is of interest how many parameters would be required for them to solve the problem based on known properties of the estimators.

As a reminder, the generalized XOR problem requires that m features in a row sum to k for the label to be 1, else the label is 0. It is an example of a complex Boolean logic problem that is useful for exploring the properties of estimators. Throughout the rest of this chapter, we will assume $k = m - 1$.

5.3.2.1 Linear Interaction Terms

Linear interaction terms are able to solve the generalized XOR problem using a fully combinatoric expansion of parameters. In other words, for $m = 3$ and $k = 2$, linear interaction terms can solve the problem using all single features, three two-way interactions and one three-way interaction. The number of parameters in the solution is $1+3+3+1 = 8$, which can be more generally expressed as follows.

$$\text{Number of parameters} = \sum_{v=0}^{m} \binom{m}{v}$$

5.3.2.2 Neural Perceptions

It can be shown that a fully connected feedforward neural network model with a number of hidden layers d will be able to draw $d + 1$ hyperplanes within the feature space in order to classify the data. Further, it can be shown that the generalized XOR problem requires m hyperplanes to solve. Therefore, the smallest network capable of solving the generalized XOR problem will have $m - 1$ hidden layers.

This is bad news for the number of parameters required to solve the problem. The number of parameters required to fit a fully connected neural network with m features and d hidden layers is as follows.

$$\text{Number of parameters} = dm^2 + d(m + 1) + 1$$

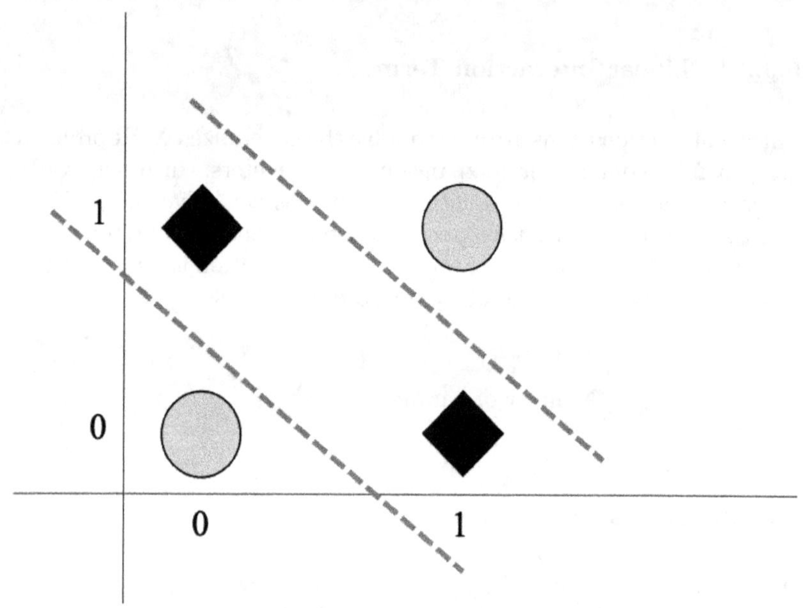

Figure 5.3: Neural network solution to classic XOR problem. In 2 dimensions, hyperplanes are lines.

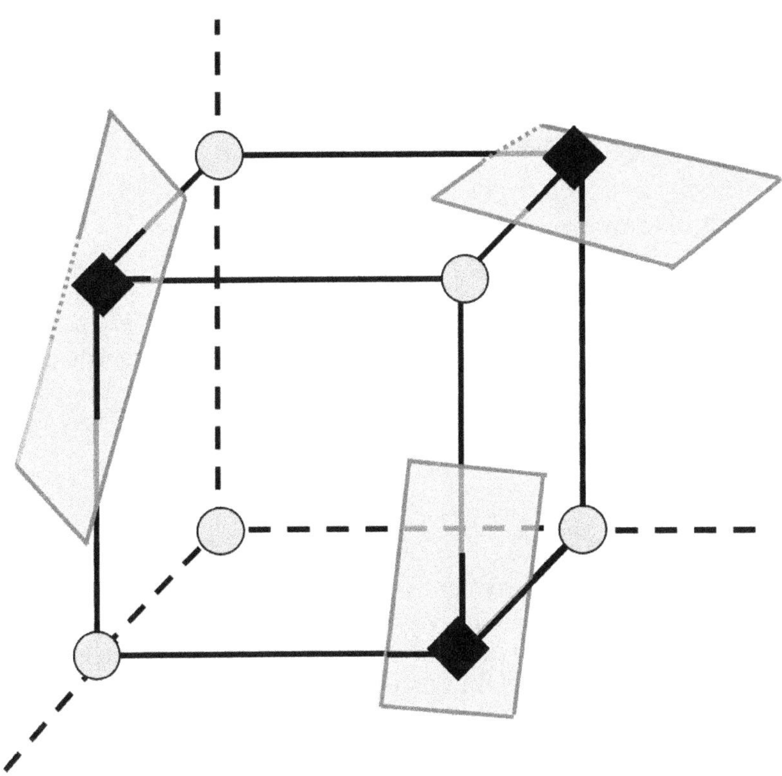

Figure 5.4: Solution to generalized XOR problem with m=3 and k=2. In 3 dimensions, hyperplanes are planes.

For $m = 3$ and $d = 2$, this suggests the network will require $2(3^2) + 2(3+1) + 1 = 27$ parameters. If we substitute out d for $m - 1$, we get the following formula for the number of parameters.

$$\text{Number of parameters} = m^3$$

This exposes a fundamental problem with neural networks. The number of parameters required is cubic with the number of useful features in complex Boolean logic problems. We will extend this result later in the chapter and compare with other estimators.

5.3.2.3   Node Splits

The number of node splits required to solve the generalized XOR problem is difficult to analytically derive. For $m = 3$, there are $n = 2^m$ possible points. A naive decision tree could classify every single point with $n - 1$ leaf splits, while an intelligent decision tree may be able to do it in fewer splits. In this case, all $n - 1$ splits are required. As such, $3 * (8 - 1) = 21$ parameters are required.

$$\text{Number of parameters} = 3(2^m - 1)$$

In practice, we will not attempt to fully describe the data, because that would result in an overfit model. Nonetheless, this is a useful yardstick for the behavior of decision trees in the presence of increasingly complex non-linear data. In this context, the number of parameters required scales exponentially with the number of useful features. If we were to add useless features into the data, the number of required parameters would not increase. This discussion provides a window into the noise-filtering capabilities of decision trees, which we will discuss further.

5.3.3   Solving the Noisy XOR Problem

As a reminder, the noisy XOR problem places the m^+ useful features with m^- useless features, where the set of useful features J_i^+ can vary

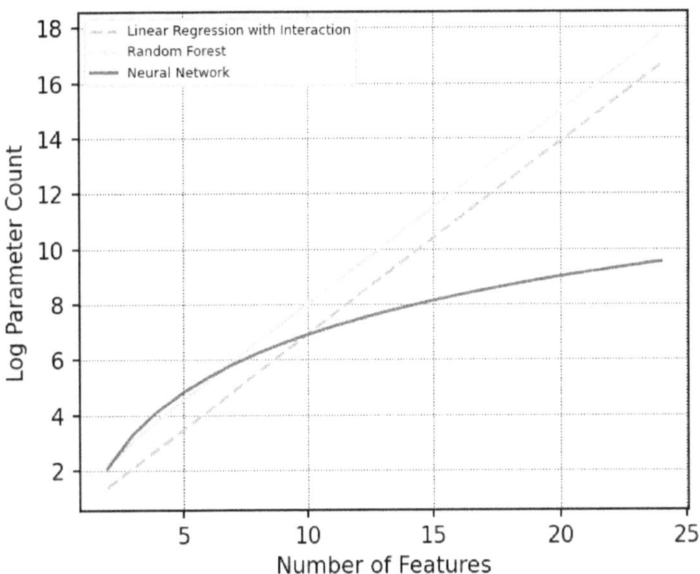

Figure 5.5: Parameter count by model for completely solving generalized XOR

from row-to-row in the training data. We designed the problem in this way because it closely resembles many financial data sets we see in the wild. In this section, we will build on the last section to study the implications of modeling this type of data with different estimators.

Recall that all the features in J_i^- are randomly uniformly distributed between zero and one, and all the features in J_i^+ have a value of either zero or one. In other words, the values in J_i^+ are extreme values. A good base estimator will have to be able to learn to identify likely extreme values, filter out likely insignificant values, then analyze patterns within the extreme values to arrive at a good estimate. If an estimator does not have this filtering capability, it cannot succeed in solving noisy XOR.

Further, noisy XOR can not be solved perfectly. There will inevitably be some irreducible error within such a data set. We know how to compute y_i in principle, but still, some noise within the data might get in the way. In other words, since the model has no foreknowledge of J_i^+, it cannot perfectly determine y_i.

5.3.3.1   Linear Interaction Terms

The noisy XOR problem requires estimators that can learn conditional effects. For example, if $x_{i,1} = 1$ and $x_{i,2} = 1$, a good estimator would be able to search for additional extreme values where $x_{i,j} = 0$ in order to make an informed estimate of y_i. A generalized linear model with interaction terms cannot accomplish this, because the ideal value of β_j or $\gamma_{j,k}$ or a higher-order interaction term would need to be dependent on the values of $x_{i,j}$ for $j \in 1, ..., m$.

Theoretically, the best available linear model would include all available interaction effects, and would have the same number of parameters as the linear model described in the previous section, which does not depend on m^+ or k.

$$\text{Number of parameters} = \sum_{v=0}^{m} \binom{m}{v}$$

5.3.3.2 Neural Perceptrons

A feedforward neural network can learn conditional effects, but it is not good at filtering out noise. In order for a neural network to filter out noise in the noisy XOR problem, it needs to learn a very specific set of hyperplanes near the boundaries of the feature space. In order for it to do that, it needs a fully connected network with depth equal to one less than the number of required hyperplanes.

Given a number of useful features m^+ and $k = m^+ - 1$, there exist $\binom{m}{m^+}$ hypercubes each with m^+ vertices with labels of $y_i = 1$, each requiring their own hyperplane to identify. Our earlier result shows that a neural network requires $h - 1$ fully connected hidden layers to identify h hyperplanes. In the terminology of our toy problem, we would require the following number of parameters.

$$\text{Number of parameters} = \left(\binom{m}{m^+} m^+ \right)^3$$

For our earlier example with $m = 6$, $m^+ = 3$, and $k = 2$, the network would require $216,000$ parameters. The construction of this problem is intentionally punishing to neural networks. Neural networks perform best when estimating naturalistic functions and shapes that benefit from regions created by multiple intersections of hyperplanes. The hyperplanes required by this problem are very discretized and unnatural in the sense that they are completely isolated and exist at the boundaries of the feature space. These characteristics make it difficult for a neural network to learn the nature of the data.

There is some potential to reduce the number of parameters by implementing an ensemble of neural networks, or a unique architecture of networks, that makes decisions by voting. We will explore this concept further when we discuss decision trees.

5.3.3.3 Node Splits

Picture how a decision tree would attempt to solve the noisy XOR problem, where the importance of one feature is dependent on the values of other features. A single decision tree cannot support the required complexity without overfitting, but an ensemble of trees can. For example, say that we want to solve the noisy XOR problem with $m = 6$, $m^+ = 3$, and $k = 2$ using an ensemble of trees.

We would want to train $\binom{m}{m^+}$ trees, each on a subset of m^+ features, in order for each tree to confidently learn the patterns against which $\sum_{j \in J_i^+} x_{i,j} = k$. In order to make predictions, we would query the predictions of all of the trees at once. If any trees returned a 1, we would know that one of the specially trained trees identified a pattern in the data, and we would classify the prediction of the ensemble as a 1. This strategy is able to nearly perfectly solve the noisy XOR problem with a known number of parameters.

In this setup, each tree would be responsible for learning all of the permutations for which $\sum_{j \in J_i^+} x_{i,j} = k$ in the data, given a unique set of features J_i^+. There are 2^m such permutations of each unique combination of features. We know from a previous result that this requires $3(2^{m^+} - 1)$ parameters. Thus, we can say that the number of parameters required to fit the noisy XOR data is as follows.

$$\text{Number of parameters} = 3\binom{m}{m^+}(2^{m^+} - 1)$$

This is necessarily much less than the corresponding fully connected neural network, because the model is being asked to learn simple bounded regions, rather than hyperplanes, in order to identify parts of the feature space where $y_i = 1$. For our earlier example with $m = 6$, $m^+ = 3$, and $k = 2$, the ensemble of trees would require 420 parameters.

5.3.4 Discussion

We have hopefully presented a sufficient analytical argument in favor of decision trees for use in a financial context. The number of parameters required to fit a model affects a number of requirements, including the size of data, the total information content of the data, and the compute

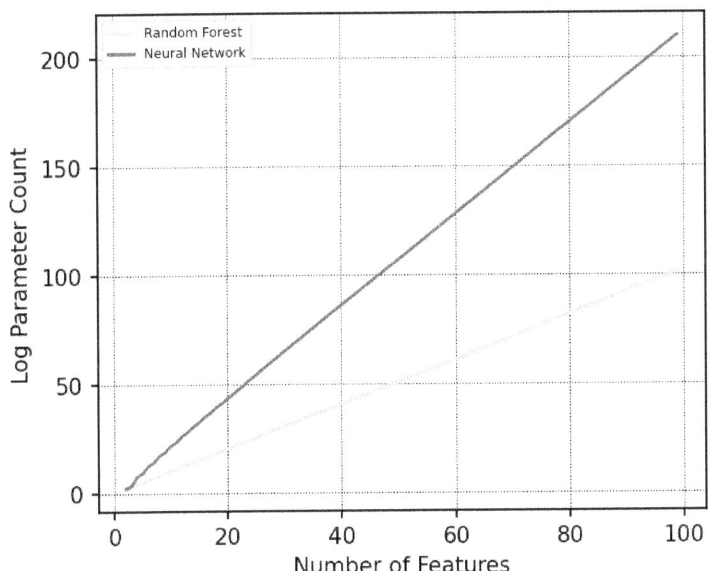

Figure 5.6: Parameter count by model for completely solving noisy XOR

time. Further, correctly specifying the model to the data affects the likelihood of convergence and the accuracy of the result.

Our core argument is that the number of parameters required to fit a neural network is too high in most financial contexts, because most financial data sets resemble the noisy XOR problem with $m > 10$ parameters. Additionally, ensembles of trees provide the necessary facilities to address the challenges of the noisy XOR problem. Conveniently, these facilities are readily provided through popular algorithms like Random Forests, Extra Trees, and Gradient Boosting Machines.

5.4   Code Appendix

See the following simulations for an applied exploration of this chapter's argument. We will start with a script to generate the sample data.

Listing 5.1: Creating sample data

```python
import numpy as np


def generate_generalized_xor_dataset(m, k):
    from itertools import product
    x_values = [i for i in product(range(2), repeat=m)]
    X = np.array(x_values)
    y_values = [int(sum(row) == k) for row in x_values]
    y = np.array(y_values)
    return X, y


def generate_vanilla_xor_dataset():
    return generate_generalized_xor_dataset(m=2, k=1)


def generate_noisy_xor_dataset(m, m_plus, k):
    # Use this as a baseline
    _X, _y = generate_generalized_xor_dataset(m_plus, k)

    # The number of columns to be randomly generated
```

```python
    random_cols = m - m_plus

    # The total rows in the result. Somewhat arbitrary.
    n_rows = _X.shape[0] * 100

    data = list()
    labels = list()
    for _ in range(n_rows):

        # Randomly select a row from _X
        source_row_idx = np.random.randint(0, _X.shape[0])
        source_row = _X[source_row_idx]

        # Build the random part of the row
        rand_row = np.random.uniform(size=(random_cols,))

        # Combine and shuffle
        out_row = np.concatenate([source_row, rand_row])
        np.random.shuffle(out_row)

        # Add result
        data.append(out_row)

        # Add corresponding random value from _y
        label = _y[source_row_index]
        labels.append(label)

    X = np.array(data)
    y = np.array(labels)

    return X, y
```

Listing 5.2: Fitting a linear model with interaction terms

```python
import numpy as np

def score_glm_predictions(X, y):
    from sklearn.preprocessing import PolynomialFeatures
    from sklearn.linear_model import LinearRegression

    # Get fully combinatoric interaction terms
    n_columns = X.shape[1]
    poly_features = PolynomialFeatures(
        degree=n_columns,
        interaction_only=True,
        include_bias=False,
    )
    X_poly = poly_features.fit_transform(X)

    # Fit the model
    lin_reg = LinearRegression()
    lin_reg.fit(X_poly, y)

    # Check equality
    y_hat = (lin_reg.predict(X_poly) > 0.5)
    y_hat = y_hat.astype('int64')
    score = np.mean(y == y_hat)

    # Compute the number of parameters
    parameters = X_poly.shape[1] + 1
    print(f'Linear model accuracy: {100*score:.1f}%')
    print(f'Linear model params: {parameters}')
```

Listing 5.3: Fitting a decision tree classifier

```python
import numpy as np

def score_forest_predictions(X, y):
    """
    To make the in-sample result realistic, we set
    min_weight_fraction_leaf to 0.001, otherwise, it would
    have 100% accuracy by definition.
    """
    from sklearn.ensemble import RandomForestClassifier
    forest_clf = RandomForestClassifier(
        n_estimators=100,
        min_weight_fraction_leaf=0.001,
    )
    forest_clf.fit(X, y)
    y_hat = forest_clf.predict(X)
    score = np.mean(y == y_hat)
    parameters = np.sum([
        est.tree_.node_count * 3 for est in \
            forest_clf.estimators_
    ])
    print(f'Random forest accuracy: {100*score:.1f}%')
    print(f'Random forest params: {parameters}')
```

Listing 5.4: Fitting a random forest classifier

```python
import numpy as np

def score_forest_predictions(X, y):
    """
    To make the in-sample result realistic, we set
    min_weight_fraction_leaf to 0.001, otherwise, it would
    have 100% accuracy by definition.
    """
    from sklearn.ensemble import RandomForestClassifier
    forest_clf = RandomForestClassifier(
        n_estimators=100,
        min_weight_fraction_leaf=0.001,
    )
    forest_clf.fit(X, y)
    y_hat = forest_clf.predict(X)
    score = np.mean(y == y_hat)
    parameters = np.sum([
        est.tree_.node_count * 3 for est in \
            forest_clf.estimators_
    ])
    print(f'Random forest accuracy: {100*score:.1f}%')
    print(f'Random forest parameters: {parameters}')
```

Listing 5.5: Fitting a neural network

```python
def score_neural_net_predictions(X, y, hyperplanes,
    parameters_only=False):
    import tensorflow as tf
    import tflearn

    def count_parameters():
        return np.sum([
            np.prod(v.shape) for v in \
                tf.compat.v1.trainable_variables()
        ])

    # Reshape data for tensorflow
    y = y.reshape(-1, 1)

    # Utility functions
    generate_weights = tflearn.initializations.uniform(
        minval=-1.0,
        maxval=1.0,
    )

    def add_layer(net, n_units):
        return tflearn.fully_connected(
            net,
            n_units=n_units,
            activation='sigmoid',
            weights_init=generate_weights,
        )

    def add_regressor(net):
        return tflearn.regression(
            net,
            optimizer='sgd', # Gradient descent
            learning_rate=0.25, # Set a fast learning rate
            loss='mean_square', # Mean-squared error
        )
```

```python
with tf.Graph().as_default():

    # Build the neural net
    net = tflearn.input_data(shape=[None, X.shape[1]])
    for _ in range(hyperplanes - 1):
        net = add_layer(net, n_units=hyperplanes)
    net = add_layer(net, n_units=1)
    net = add_regressor(net)
    model = tflearn.DNN(net, tensorboard_verbose=0)

    # Skip the fit step in case it is hopeless
    if parameters_only:
        parameters = count_parameters()
        print(f'Neural net params:{parameters}')
        print(f'Neural net skipping fit.')
        return

    # A good estimate of the necessary training epochs
    n_epochs = (m-1) * 10000

    # Fit the model
    model.fit(
        X, y,
        n_epoch=n_epochs,
        snapshot_epoch=False,
    )

    # Check equality
    y_hat = (model.predict(X) > 0.5).astype('int64')
    score = np.mean(y_hat == y)

    # Compute the number of parameters
    parameters = count_parameters()
    print(f'Neural net accuracy: {100*score:.1f}%')
    print(f'Neural net params: {parameters}')
```

Listing 5.6: Running the experiment

```python
# Basic XOR problem
print('\n\nFitting basic XOR problem ...')
m, k = 2, 1
X_vanilla, y_vanilla = generate_vanilla_xor_dataset()
score_glm_predictions(X_vanilla, y_vanilla)
score_tree_predictions(X_vanilla, y_vanilla)
score_forest_predictions(X_vanilla, X_vanilla)
score_neural_net_predictions(
    X_vanilla,
    y_vanilla,
    hyperplanes=m,
)

# Generalized XOR problem
print('\n\nFitting generalized XOR problem ...')
m, k = 4, 3
X_general, y_general = \
    generate_generalized_xor_dataset(m, k)

score_glm_predictions(X_general, y_general)
score_tree_predictions(X_general, y_general)
score_forest_predictions(X_general, X_general)
score_neural_net_predictions(
    X_general,
    y_general,
    hyperplanes=m,
)

# Noisy XOR problem
print('\n\nFitting noisy XOR problem ...')
from math import factorial as f
a_choose_b = lambda a, b: f(a) // f(b) // f(a - b)

m, m_plus, k = 6, 3, 2
X_noisy, y_noisy = \
    generate_noisy_xor_dataset(m, m_plus, k)
```

```
score_glm_predictions(X_noisy, y_noisy)
score_tree_predictions(X_noisy, y_noisy)
score_forest_predictions(X_noisy, y_noisy)
score_neural_net_predictions(
    X_noisy,
    y_noisy,
    hyperplanes=a_choose_b(m, m_plus) * m_plus,
    parameters_only=True,
)
```

Chapter 6

Better Features

This chapter will discuss how to compute better financial features. We will focus not just on features that *ought to* contribute to investment performance, but features that *tend to* contribute to investment performance. Our core argument will be based on the fact that your asset is only worth as much as another investor is willing to pay for it. As such, when developing a model to predict the future price of an asset, you will want to prioritize features that other investors think are important.

I am alluding to two specific theories that refer to the ability of investor expectations and preferences to drive prices to persistent disequilibria. The first is the "The Keynesian Beauty Contest", where John Maynard Keynes compared the stock market to a contest between judges. Given a beauty contest with one hundred faces to choose from, the winning judge is the one that can pick the most popular face among all judges, rather than the face he may personally find the most attractive. The second is the "Theory of Reflexivity" in finance, which George Soros popularized by proposing the existence of self-reinforcing feedback loops between investor expectations and intrinsic valuation factors. Readers are encouraged to seek a deeper understanding of these concepts as a companion to this chapter.

In the context of financial machine learning, these theories suggest that the best model is not one that understands companies, but one that understands markets. This chapter will discuss a few featurization techniques that respect the expectations of investors, rational or otherwise, over pure analytical finance principles.

6.1   Non-material Growth

Let us pause and contemplate the world of investment banking. An investment bank provides many services to its clients, but let us consider a company sale. In the same way a family hires a real estate agent to market and sell their home, a company hires an investment bank to market and sell it.

In the world of investment banking, potential buyers are sophisticated companies or investors with several industry experts and advisors. As such, marketing a company to a potential buyer is not as simple as giving the financial statements a fresh coat of paint and highlighting some impressive performance metrics. The bankers prepare in-depth materials summarizing the company's operations, financial performance, and future growth trajectory. Interested parties will use the marketing materials and their own due diligence to calculate potential returns before investing in the company.

Imagine, for example, that a mature company with a stable $10m in quarterly revenue made a one-time marketing investment of $5m in Q1. After accounting for other expenses, the company's net income in Q1 was a paltry $100K. Due to the non-recurring nature of the marketing investment, SG&A decreased by $5mm in Q2. Unfortunately, the marketing campaign was a catastrophic failure and had no impact on revenue. Still, their net income in Q2 was reported as $5.1m.

Let us think about how this appears to a naive machine learning model. On paper, the company's net income grew 5,000% QoQ. Further, this net income growth is likely the best reported across all publicly traded companies in the industry. Accordingly, it would be very easy for a naive machine learning model make an unwise prediction about the company's future performance. Further, we would prefer that our machine learning model not encode any information like this during training.

Notwithstanding this contrived example, there are numerous ways a company can create the appearance of extraordinary financial performance using non-recurring methods that do not correspond to intrinsic business success. Sophisticated investors know that such anomalous growth is non-repeatable and is likely the result of a one-time investment, an accounting rule, or an unexpected event. During due diligence, a potential buyer will either normalize the result by analyzing pro-forma financial statements or exclude the result by labeling it as as non-material. This 5,000% growth would be labeled non-material and excluded when reviewing the investment. Accordingly, machine learning engineers should normalize or exclude non-material observations when featurizing data to avoid training a model that makes unrealistic predictions about future price performance.

Financial data scientists are tasked with the challenge of quantitatively identifying all instances of non-material growth in order to treat them appropriately in their machine learning models. See Table 6.1 for some examples of net income numbers reported in two adjacent financial quarters for eight companies.

Company	Q1 ($mm)	Q2 ($mm)
A	10	20
B	-10	0
C	-10	20
D	-20	-10
E	-10	-20
F	0	20
G	-20	10
H	10	-30

Table 6.1: Net income for companies in first and second quarters

The remainder of this section will discuss some methods of featurizing net income growth intelligently, and then speculate on ways in which this problem can be addressed on a larger time horizon. The goal of featurization is to give the machine learning model a common sense idea of what is good and bad. In other words, we need to rank companies A-H from best to worst in terms of net income growth. To do this, we can consider the three return calculations listed below.

$$\text{I. } y - x \qquad \text{II. } \frac{y}{x} - 1 \qquad \text{III. } \frac{y - x}{(|x| + |y|)/2}$$

For our example, we can apply these formulas to assess the resultant ranking and determine the validity of our formula. Table 6.2 summarizes the return calculations on the net income figures, where columns II and III are expressed as proportions.

Company	Q1 ($mm)	Q2 ($mm)	I ($mm)	II	III
A	10	20	10	1.0	0.66
B	-10	0	10	-1.0	2.00
C	-10	20	30	-3.0	2.00
D	-20	-10	10	-0.5	0.66
E	-10	-20	-10	1.0	-0.66
F	0	20	20	∞	2.00
G	-20	10	30	-4.0	2.00
H	10	-30	-40	-4.0	-2.00

Table 6.2: Various attempts at measuring net income growth

A machine learning model would have a hard time learning anything using formula I as dollar values are not particularly helpful on a standalone basis. The companies may vary in size, and a $30mm increase may be less significant than a $10mm loss. A machine learning model applying formula II would be unhelpful as it would inappropriately encode information about non-material growth, causing it to make erratic predictions based on false patterns.

In terms of ranking companies from best to worst, formula III is the most logical albeit unsatisfying in practice. The third formula still fails to draw on any contextual information. Further, it treats very different quarter-over-quarter performances as equal where it likely should not. In practice, we can look at longer time horizons, industry benchmarks, and other contextual information when developing formulas that normalize non-material growth.

This example illustrates how featurization is a fundamentally artful problem with no precise solution. It also reinforces the idea that machine learning engineers can create highly differentiated and effective models by intelligently addressing this problem.

6.2 Keynesian Beauty Contest

It is no secret that technical indicators do not work in isolation. For example, there is no single configuration of Bollinger Bands that consistently generates profitable signals. This fact causes many machine learning engineers to write off technical indicators as unhelpful or worthless to their strategies. In many cases they are right. This section will offer an argument as to why they might be wrong.

Let us re-examine technical indicators in the context of the Keynesian Beauty Contest and the Theory of Reflexivity. In the context of these theories, it is unimportant which technical indicators reveal real patterns in trading activity. It is more important to consider which technical indicators *are thought to* reveal patterns in trading activity.

In a Keynesian Beauty Contest, the most popular technical indicators will generate the best trading signals, provided that enough market participants are relying on technical trading signals. For sake of argument, let $k_i \in (-\infty, \infty)$ represent the direction and size of the trade of market participant $i \in 1, ..., n$. Assume that all trading in the short-term occurs based on technical signals, and that market participant i is using one of many available technical indicators $j \in J$. Some market participants may be using the same indicator, but they do not know this with certainty. As such, j_i will represent the subset of all $i \in 1, ..., n$ market participants that are using indicator j.

The sum of all capital trading against indicator j is the following.

$$K_j = \sum_{i \in j_i} k_i$$

Further, the total of participating capital is the following.

$$K = \sum_{j \in J} K_j = \sum_{i=1}^{n} k_i$$

Consider a technical indicator f_j that generates a time series $z_{t,j} = f_j(y_t)$ called the indicator line. The can be any technical indicator that generates any sort of time series. For example, this can be an RSI line, an Accumulation-Distribution line, or a Bollinger Percent-B line.

Further, consider the signal-generating function $w_{t,j} = g_j(z_t)$. This function has a range of $[-1, +1]$, and its sole responsibility is to translate the time series z_t into a trading signal. A signal of -1 would trigger the investor to sell all of his investment of size k_i and a positive $+1$ would trigger the investor to buy shares worth a total of k_i. A signal of 0 would indicate no action.

Many popular signal-generating functions will only produce values in the set $\{-1, 0, +1\}$. For example, a moving average crossover would generate a signal of $+1$ when there is a crossover, -1 when there is a crossunder, and 0 otherwise. Other signal-generating functions will generate continuous values that trigger the investor to adjust his net-long or net-short exposure over time. Many machine learning models perform in the latter fashion.

According to the Keynesian Beauty Contest model of market trading, the following is a formula for the optimal indicator line, w'_t.

$$w'_t = \frac{1}{K} \sum_{j \in J} K_j w_{t,j}$$

In the above equation, w'_t represents the net dollar volume actively trading the asset expressed as a proportion of all capital actively trading the asset. In other words, if 30% of the money being traded was following a Bollinger Band entry model, and a Bollinger Band setup occurred, the indicator would tell you to buy the stock in anticipation of an influx of demand from Bollinger Band users. In the language of the beauty contest, the technical indicator is the criteria the trader is using to quantify beauty. The most beautiful stock, therefore, would be the one that simultaneously fulfills multiple popular criteria for beauty.

This concept translates very elegantly to a few major concepts in machine learning, all of which provide an opportunity to model investor consensus as determined by different preference criteria.

1. Weak learners
2. Voting classifiers
3. Ensemble models

For example, if you imagine that every market participant is a decision tree, then the prediction step of a random forest classifier looks very similar to the equation for w'_t. In other words, a collection of decision trees mimics the collection of individual actors in the market. Examining all of the outputs of the decision trees simultaneously, as a random forest does, will allow us to uncover rare instances where many market participants are in agreement about what to trade and how.

6.3 Theory of Reflexivity

So far, we have argued that the most useful technical indicators are the most popular ones, rather than the most sophisticated ones. We will extend this concept to the Theory of Reflexivity to analyze instances where movements in w'_t can create positive feedback loops with the underlying price y_t as time progresses.

It is widely appreciated that the original mathematical formulation of the Theory of Reflexivity is not very rigorous. As such, our definition with regards to our argument about technical indicators will look only thematically similar.

Given that w'_t is the optimal technical indicator, we will assume it is proportional to $\Delta y_t = y_t - y_{t-1}$ in the following way.

$$\Delta y_{t+1} \propto w'_t$$

Expanding the equation in terms of y_t, we get the following, where $h_k(\cdot) = g_j(f_j(\cdot))$ represents the composition of the signal-generating function and the indicator function.

$$\Delta y_{t+1} \propto \sum_{j \in J} \left[K_j * h_j(y_t) \right]$$

Generally, we can describe K_j as the popularity of indicator j, which acts on the price series $y_t \in 1, ..., t$ via $h_j(\cdot)$. In the above equation, K_j is bounded between zero and ∞, and $h_j(\cdot)$ is bounded between negative one and positive one. By studying the characteristics of the various functions $h_j(\cdot)$, we can understand the types of feedback loops that exist in financial markets.

We will start by categorizing all of the functions $h_j(\cdot)$ for $j \in J$ as either momentum or reversal indicators. Momentum indicators are those that treat increasing prices as evidence that prices will continue to increase, and vice-versa. Examples include moving average crosses and Bollinger Band breakouts. Reversal indicators are those that treat increasing prices as evidence that prices will soon decrease, and vice-versa. Examples including Relative Strength Index reversals and Bollinger Band reversals.

Mathematically, if $h_j(\cdot)$ was a pure momentum indicator, it would be a monotonically increasing function. Conversely, if $h_j(\cdot)$ was a pure reversal indicator, it would be a monotonically decreasing function. If we separate out momentum and reversal indicators into groups J^+ and J^-, respectively, we can expand the prior equation. First, let us define $h'_j(\cdot) = -h_j(\cdot)$ for $j \in J^-$ as the momentum version of $h_j(\cdot)$. This effectively converts every function in the equation into a monotonically increasing one, which allows us to do some creative math on the resultant terms.

$$\Delta y_{t+1} \propto \sum_{j \in J^+} \left[K_j * h_j(y_t) \right] - \sum_{j \in J^-} \left[K_j * h'_j(y_t) \right]$$

For the remainder of this argument, we will assume all $h_j(\cdot)$ have a similar sensitivity to price movements. In other words, we will assume that the absolute value of the derivatives of all $h_j(\cdot)$ with respect to y_t are similar. This allows us to assume $|h_j(y_t) - h_j(y_{t-1})|$ is constant across all $j \in J$ and proportional to Δy_t.

Given this assumption, the momentum-biased actively traded capital can be denoted $K^+ = \sum_{j \in J^+} K_j$ and the reversal-biased actively traded capital can be denoted $K^- = \sum_{j \in J^-} K_j$. Utilizing our new assumptions, we can take the difference operator of the equation for Δy_{t+1} to achieve the following.

$$\Delta^2 y_{t+1} \propto \Delta y_t (K^+ - K^-)$$

This equation has powerful implications. It states that the second derivative of price, which can be thought of as the pricing pressure, is proportional to the previous change in price, multiplied by the net momentum bias, $K^+ - K^-$.

Let us examine the net momentum bias further. If $K^+ - K^-$ is positive, it indicates that there is more actively traded capital in the market that favors momentum patterns. If it is negative, it indicates that there is more actively traded capital in the market that favors reversal patterns.

The above formula for $\Delta^2 y_{t+1}$ provides a simple model for explaining how the principle of reflexivity can cause prices to skyrocket or crash in a seemingly illogical way. In other words, violent price swings only occur when the net momentum bias is large and persistent. When it is large and persistent, the only thing that can be assured is volatility.

If the net momentum bias was time-invariant, prices would skyrocket out of control permanently. In practice, K^+ and K^- will vary across time as investor preferences and expectations change. The sum of all actively traded capital in the market, K, will also vary across time as interest in that particular asset changes.

Much like Soros's original mathematical model of the Theory of Reflexivity, this model is meant to serve as a thought experiment and mental framework to help us understand how prices are driven entirely by investor expectations and preferences. Readers are encouraged to think about events and experiences in their financial trading careers where they have witnessed some of the following.

- Increasing asset prices were seen as proof-of-value of the asset, rather than evidence that it is overvalued, causing prices to continue to increase.
- Increasing asset prices created advantageous business opportunities that would not have otherwise been available, causing prices to continue to increase.
- Decreasing asset prices were seen as proof-of-valuelessness of the asset, rather than evidence that it is undervalued, causing prices to continue to decrease.
- Decreasing asset prices caused managers or administrators to take corrective actions that served as confirmatory evidence that the asset is of low value, causing asset prices to further decrease.

These are all instances where the net momentum bias is strong, potentially for an extended period of time.

6.4   Conclusion

In this chapter, we gave a few arguments as to why the best features are those that other investors consider valuable. Ultimately, your ability to make a profit depends on another investor's ability to value your asset above your purchase price. Therefore, it is wise to consider what that investor wants. Readers are encouraged to think about this as they engineer features for financial machine learning models.